FROM PAIN TO PEACE

How Trauma and Tragedy Teach Us Compassion and Wisdom

MEL HARKRADER PINE

Prospecta Press

Paperback ISBN 978-1-63226-178-6
eBook ISBN 978-1-63226-179-3
Limited edition hardcover ISBN 978-163226-180-9

Published by
Prospecta Press
PO Box 3131
Westport, CT 06880
www.prospectapress.com

Book and cover design by Alexia Garaventa
Manufactured in the United States of America

This book is dedicated to the memory of Alice, Eddie, Margaret, Barry, Marilyn, Alex, Thomas, and all whose traumatic deaths teach us compassion and wisdom.

Sorrow comes in great waves . . . but it rolls over us, and though it may almost smother us it leaves us on the spot, and we know that if it is strong we are stronger, inasmuch as it passes and we remain. It wears us, uses us, but we wear it and use it in return; and it is blind, whereas we after a manner see.

—Henry James, letter to Grace Norton, July 28, 1883

CONTENTS

PROLOGUE

I've been to the depths of sorrow where I'm crying on the floor and I don't know what to do. Thankfully, I had community that I could call, and someone would come over and hold my hand and be there with me . . .

The speaker was my friend Chelsea Waves, a death doula, grief companion, and lucid dreaming guide. My junior in age by four and a half decades, she has the wisdom and compassion gained from two decades of caring for a mother with schizophrenia whose seventh suicide attempt was successful. Chelsea was answering my question, during a podcast interview, about how trauma can grant the blessing of equanimity, along with wisdom and compassion. She continued:

Through that, I am able to connect with other people who are having these experiences of deep, deep, deep sadness. I'm grateful that I was able to meet that moment for myself and go to those kinds of places.

At the same time, I've had to cultivate the equanimity that you're speaking to, and through my own yearning to grow I have been able to see and look back on my traumas and say:

My mother's dying, that was a rite of passage. That was her gift to me so that I can live my life freely. If she hadn't died, my life would be very different.

For me, moving through these lessons in my life brought the growth and understanding that led me to a bigger context.

That exchange planted the seed for me to share my long road of tragedies and healing in this spiritual memoir.

INTRODUCTION

We all experience suffering and trauma, though the circumstances that deliver them differ for each of us. Some of us never recover from the pain; some barely recover; many recover stronger. In this book, I use my trauma-punctuated life as an illustration of the spiritual gifts that tragedies bring. They help us deepen our compassion and wisdom.

They have enabled me to live the final stage of my life in joy.

That you're reading or listening to this Introduction demonstrates the universality of pain as well as the desire to find a path to something better. We will never escape losses and traumas, but we can find in our pain a path to peace and spiritual wholeness.

Although the circumstances that deliver suffering may be expected life events, such as the death of a parent or a child's departure from home, they often sink us for a time under a wave of sadness. Other circumstances that deliver pain come without warning—a phone call announces the violent death of a loved one; a terrorist bomb explodes fifty yards away from us. We call it trauma when the resulting pain feels too great to handle.

Paradoxically, in the right environment, the deeper the suffering we endure, the further we may go toward spiritual wholeness. Losing our innocence, our support systems, our loved ones, and maybe even some of our memories leaves a void longing to be filled. If we begin with compassion for ourselves and then summon compassion for others, we can fill the void with love.

If that sounds too new-agey for you, it comes from someone whose life has been punctuated by violent and gritty crises. But don't take my word for it. Here's a quotation from a Roman Catholic professor of spiritual formation about a moment of clarity that came to him after hours of hallucinations and violence as he was locked in the padded cell of an asylum: "I was but a tiny molecule of a boundless sea that holds, without judgment or distortion, all things in the reflection of its unequivocal love."

Dr. Frank Rogers Jr. was just beginning on a path toward grace that would take him decades to achieve (though never to a complete recovery) after a childhood of sexual abuse so awful and persistent that it deserves the adjective "unspeakable." He had the courage to write of it in his memoir, *Cradled in the Arms of Compassion: A Spiritual Journey from Trauma to Recovery*, which I discovered as I did the research for this book. I suppose it takes considerable chutzpah to begin my own spiritual memoir with a zillion-star review of another, but do consider reading his—as well as mine, of course.

Dr. Rogers showed up on my screen as I searched for academic substantiation of my intuitive observation that those who suffer severe traumas early in life are often predisposed to experience enhanced compassion and spiritual fulfillment later in life.

Because his book is intensely intimate, I'll call the author by his first name, Frank. He's a professor of Spiritual Formation and Narrative Pedagogy at the Claremont School of Theology and a codirector of the Center for Engaged Compassion.

What's remarkable about Frank's extensive research is that much of it has been conducted on himself as he explored his feelings during long and painful decades following a childhood that few of us could face head-on, as he needed to. With the strong motivation to heal himself and also help others to heal, he tells his story in detail.

In 2007, I shared with a coworker named Valerie a thought I had never explored out loud. She was exceptionally compassionate, and after I learned that she had an adult brother with a profound developmental disorder that left him unable to speak, feed himself, or walk, I said to Valerie, "You know, I see you as a compassionate person, and over the years I've met others who grew up with disabled siblings. Do you think that contributes to the compassion?"

With no hesitation, Valerie replied, "Absolutely. I saw how my mother loved and cared for him, and I joined her. We had to anticipate his needs, feed him, understand his efforts to communicate, change his diapers, and make his life worth living."

I noticed also that particularly compassionate people I met often had experienced a traumatic loss early in their lives. I now understand that all trauma leaves one needing to care for someone—most significantly, oneself.

Chelsea Waves, whom you met in the Prologue, cared for her mother, who suffered from schizophrenia over two decades and through six suicide attempts before finally losing her life on the seventh. By learning to care for both her mother and herself, Chelsea developed a wealth of profound wisdom as well as compassion by the time she reached her thirties.

In my previous books, I combined didactic prose with anecdotes and bits of memoir from my life, with a goal of teaching Buddhism in a conversational, personal way. That led me to better understand how trauma, compassion, and spiritual development wove together in my life. My discussions with Chelsea led me to think about a next book written entirely as a memoir, for anyone, regardless of their spiritual path, who wanted to read about reacting to life crises as spiritual gifts. In that book I would mention only enough about Buddhism to explain how it helped me.

Before starting to write, though, I needed to answer a question: Did any academic research support my observation of a relationship between trauma, compassion, and spiritual development? I asked two AI platforms to find published studies on the subject and learned that the answer was *yes, indeed*. They each provided lots of examples.

One platform listed among its results an exhaustive study that an academic had done on his own history of severe trauma and recovery from it. I found it interesting that Frank's book made the list. Although I was intrigued, I realized that a spiritual memoir isn't what one thinks of as "academic research." Frank's book wasn't peer reviewed and published by a journal, as the others were. It contained no statistical analyses, though the others did.

I bought the e-book and started reading. I recalled that an African American Baptist minister I once met had told me that he and I were "brothers from different mothers." I wouldn't use that phrase about Frank, but as I perused his book my feeling about him was similar almost immediately. We are indeed brothers from vastly different religious backgrounds who share similar spiritual truths, arrived at through trauma and recovery. We both went through the trying process of reliving our pasts to write spiritual memoirs that we hope will help others.

Once I began reading Frank's book, I knew I'd have to complete it before finishing this one. So, as I painfully relived and wrote of my traumas and the path they led me to, I shared his reliving through the words in his own book. Here were several highlights:

- One man had grown up in a Conservative Jewish household and practiced Rimé (ecumenical) Buddhism after having experienced severe nonsexual violent traumas throughout his life.
- Another man, who grew up Christian, practiced post-Vatican II Roman Catholicism after having suffered severe and prolonged sexual traumas in childhood.
- One author relived and wrote of his path to peace while reading the other's account of his own traumas and path to peace.
- Both authors felt motivated to share their pain and examples of their eventual healing, for the benefit of others.

I read Frank's last chapters just before I wrote the end of my first draft. Here are two quotations from the final sections of his book:

> *I know that my heart is one with God's . . . My heart too beats with compassion. When I am fused with the sacred care that permeates all things, I am restored to myself.*
>
> *In the lap of* [*a Madonna's*] *tender care, all may not be well. But it all will be held.*

Now that I've read Frank's book and completed mine, I see the same story expressed in two spiritual languages. Here's my hypothesis:

- Pain is universal.
- The circumstances that deliver pain are different for every person.
- The rituals and languages that help us transform the pain into a condition of peace also differ.
- The core elements of that path are universal.

Whatever caused pain for you, readers, however slowly or abruptly it came over you, whether via the spiritual path you follow or lack of one you can acknowledge your own suffering and ultimately let it help you toward peace—what some might call *a state of grace*.

I was moved to write this book because the unusually large number of traumas I've been through, along with my experiences of psychotherapy and spiritual practice, have taught me how to live in joy. If reading my story gives you hope, I feel it will have been worth the effort I put into writing it! If it also serves as impetus or support for your spiritual path, even better.

While I wouldn't choose to live through my traumas again, each one opened wider the aperture of my heart. In that sense, they were a gift. In the chapters that follow, I'll describe those traumas and try to convey how they worked, alongside my spiritual practice, to awaken me to a life filled with compassion, spiritual wholeness, and joy.

By definition, a memoir falls into the category of nonfiction. I've done extensive research to confirm that the memories I relate in this volume align with actual recorded events, but of course memories are faulty re-creations of the past. I've added a description occasionally, even if I'm not certain of its aptness, and I also make no claim that I've accurately remembered the exact words spoken by me or others. Throughout, I've done my best to write honestly about what happened. I've changed the names of some people whose lives deserve to be kept private, but everyone I mention is real. Everyone I write about is as I remember him or her.

A FEW WORDS ABOUT LANGUAGE

It's not a huge and popular club, but I'm among those fighting racism by challenging certain racial designations. Genetically, I'm more than 99 percent Ashkenazi Jewish, and have no problem claiming that heritage. But is there a Jewish race, and am I part of it? I don't think so.

Where the idea of race goes completely off the tracks is the way we use "white" and "black" in the United States to define groups we call "races." First, there are no people who actually have white skin except for albinos, and no people exist with truly black skin. Second, even if we accept the social construct of white and black groups, the gene pools are 99.9 percent identical. I'm not advocating color blindness, but in my other writings I have used quotation marks around "white" and "black" when applying them as group designations to make it clear that they are social constructs and not "races." In this book, I've dropped that convention, but in my heart I've added invisible quotation marks.

Also, when it comes to race, some words that were commonly accepted in the 1960s and 1970s are now considered unskillful or prejudiced, even hostile. In this book, I've used "ghetto" for black as well as Jewish segregated communities, and I've used "Negro" on one occasion where its need will be obvious.

CHAPTER 1

EARLY LESSONS IN IMPERMANENCE

Minnie, get my slippers!

From the carpeted floor, the dog, a black-and-white rescue, bigger than a Chihuahua but smaller than a terrier, sprinted up the stairs. She returned in minutes and dropped my Uncle Eddie's slippers at his feet. At seven, I was astounded, but not enough to get me over my fear of dogs.

Minnie wasn't named for her size but for the Cab Calloway song "Minnie the Moocher," which had sold more than a million copies twenty years earlier. Along with Yiddish, midcentury pop music served as a language in my extended family, which consisted of my maternal grandmother, her five children, and their families, all of us living in Philadelphia.

Bubbe was the only one of my grandparents who had lived long enough for my birth. On this winter Sunday, my father drove her, my mother, and me in his 1951 Chevrolet Bel Air to visit Uncle Eddie's family in the Oak Lane neighborhood.

You could call Eddie the patriarch of the Pinsky family. Although not the oldest, he was the most successful of Bubbe's children in the "new country." He lived in the nicest house, had the best career, and considered the jazz clarinetist Benny Goodman a friend. His wife, Margaret, was fashionable—at least by Jewish-immigrant standards. Eddie was an imposing figure: tall, good-natured, kind, and warm. He cried at bar mitzvahs.

Uncle Eddie and Aunt Margaret had three children. Carl and Martin were six and five years older than me. Barry was the closest I had to an age-mate in the family tree, just five months older. With more social grace than I had, he invited me to play with him in the basement, where Martin, more of a loner, had built a cardboard fort in one corner. Barry and I weren't allowed to touch Martin's place of retreat and refuge.

Barry had his mother's artistic bent and tried to help me draw, but it was hopeless. In later years, he won a scholarship to the Philadelphia College of Art. To this day, I can't even sign my name clearly.

My father, known in the new country as Jack, had immigrated in 1921. My grandmother, known in the new country as Dora, came here with her husband, Morris, around the turn of the twentieth century. They came from *shtetls* (Jewish settlements) in the Prushin-Shereshov (pronounced *prushina-shershov*) region of what's now Belarus.

Dvereleah (Dora), born around 1875, grew up in a variation of indentured servitude. Her father, Mortra-Beryl, stayed home studying the Talmud while his wife did her best to sell staples from a pushcart. They couldn't afford to feed Dvereleah, so they gave her to a family with a disabled son. She cared for the boy and got to eat his leftovers.

I knew nothing about that when Bubbe was a member of the household. She moved in with us when I was born—to care for the *yingele* (young one), so called because I was the youngest on my branch of the family tree. My brother, Stanley, known as Ginger because of his hair color, was fifteen when I was born, and my sister, Marilyn, eleven. Because my mother, Fannie, felt overwhelmed and embarrassed to have a child at nearly forty, my Yiddish-speaking grandmother became a key caregiver.

A story I never heard is how Dvereleah met her husband in the old country. They must have been lonely souls. Both had been cast off from their families. Dvereleah's parents couldn't afford to feed her. Maisha-Yudel (Morris), as best I can tell, was an extramarital son of Shalom Yisrael Pinsky. He bore the Pinsky name but was not accepted into the family.

As an eyewitness told me, Maishe-Yudel and Dvereleah lost a child to starvation before they immigrated to the United States. Once here, Morris gave Dora five children and otherwise spent his time drinking himself to his death, which came in 1926 before he turned fifty.

Dora and her children—Sophie, then twenty-three; Harry, twenty-two; Fannie, nineteen; Eddie, thirteen; and Izzy, eleven—all made it through the Great Depression.

My father, called Yankel in the old country, was born in the same region in 1898. His father was prosperous until pogroms, wars, and military occupations led to famine and starvation. Jack didn't live long enough to share with me why and how he made the journey from Prushin-Shereshov to New York City. My research a half century after his death determined that before he left, he saw German soldiers chain his father to a plow to grow crops to feed troops on the Eastern Front of the First World War.

In 1921, Jack left to join three or four siblings who were already here. I don't know how long his parents lived, but the brother and sister he left behind tidily married a brother and sister from the Kantorowitz family. In October 1942, the Nazis shot Jack's sister, brother-in-law, and their three children to death as they hid in an apartment. The following year, his brother, sister-in-law, and their two children were taken by cattle car to Auschwitz-Birkenau, where they were killed. When I was born in 1946, I had lost two uncles, two aunts, and five cousins to genocide.

I haven't mentioned my paternal grandfather's name. It's Shalom Yisrael Pinsky, my maternal great-grandfather. I've heard no explanation of how it happened, but after Jack immigrated, he visited the half brother their father had disowned and married his daughter Fannie in 1926. So I have only one side to my family—Pinsky—except that shortly after his arrival, a relative advised my father to take a less-Jewish-sounding name. So Yankel Yussel Pinsky became Jack Pine before he married my mother.

Jack and Fannie's first child, Martin, lived only a year and died in 1930. Ginger was born in 1931 and Marilyn in 1935. The family moved from New York to Philadelphia to be closer to Bubbe and save on expenses by sharing a house with relatives. They were content with their family of four, and during this period my mother developed some, well, frigidity and prudishness. Then a long-distance call in August 1945 stirred some excitement. "Ruthie had her baby, a boy. Come see him!"

My father's sister in New York City was announcing that her grandchild Bobby had been born. Jack and Fannie left Ginger and Marilyn with the Philadelphia relatives, hopped into my father's car, and drove to see the baby. They didn't pack condoms, and I guess the joy of Bobby's birth got my mother over her coldness.

Few people know the reason they were born. I'm one of them.

The science of epigenetics is fundamentally changing how we understand inheritance. The word means "above" or "on top of" genetics. Your personal DNA sequence stays the same. You're not getting new genes or changing existing ones. Instead, chemical tags get attached to your DNA or to the proteins that package it. These tags act like dimmer switches, turning genes up or down without changing the underlying code.

The classic example is the Dutch Hunger Winter of 1944–45. Nazi forces blockaded the western Netherlands, creating a famine that killed about twenty thousand people. Pregnant women who lived through it gave birth to children with higher rates of obesity, diabetes, and heart disease—not surprising, given the prenatal malnutrition. But their grandchildren, born decades later to well-fed mothers, showed similar health issues. The trauma of starvation had marked multiple generations.

While it takes many generations for our genetic structure to change in response to our environment, the regulation of genes can shift because of experience, and those regulatory changes can sometimes be inherited. This happens in feast as well as famine.

Research in Swedish historical records found that if a male child experienced feast conditions right before puberty, then later had children and grandchildren, his grandsons would face increased mortality rates from cardiovascular disease and diabetes. If he faced famine during that same developmental window, his grandsons lived longer. The timing mattered—puberty, pregnancy, and early childhood seem to be critical windows when environmental conditions can leave lasting marks.

Animal studies have made this even clearer. Researchers can breed mice that are genetically identical—clones, essentially—yet that show wildly different traits, depending on what their mothers or grandmothers experienced. Stress, diet, toxins, even how much a mother mouse licks her pups—many factors can create epigenetic changes that affect behavior and health across generations.

Most epigenetic marks get erased between generations. If they didn't, every generation would carry the accumulated baggage of every ancestor's experience. But some marks slip through, particularly those established during critical developmental periods.

Studies of Holocaust survivors and their children suggest that trauma can leave epigenetic adaptation signatures. Researchers found altered stress hormone regulation in the children of survivors, particularly those whose mothers were pregnant during the Holocaust. The sample sizes are small and the findings debated, but if confirmed, this means that historical trauma may have biological consequences that reach into future regulation of stress hormones as well as metabolic processes.

While I learned early on that the Holocaust had taken lives in my extended family, I didn't inherit the effects of that in the womb. I *did*, however, inherit a family history of pogroms and starvation, and possibly even my mother's ambivalence about my existence.

May 23, 1956—my tenth birthday—came and went without a party or a present. Fannie was hospitalized, recovering from a heart attack, and Jack was barely managing to run the family business. He had spent forty-seven days in the same hospital after a severe attack of his own less than a year earlier.

Three decades later, I began learning core Buddhist concepts, one of which is impermanence. The Buddha put it succinctly: "Whatever has the nature of arising has the nature of ceasing."

Ajahn Chah, a twentieth-century influential Thai teacher, used this story to illustrate impermanence:

> *One day some people came to the master and asked: How can you be happy in a world of such impermanence, where you cannot protect your loved ones from harm, illness, or death? The master held up a glass and said: "Someone gave me this glass. It holds my water admirably and it glistens in the sunlight. I touch it and it rings! One day the wind may blow it off the shelf, or my elbow may knock it from the table. I know this glass is already broken, so I enjoy it—incredibly."*

In May 1956, I learned about impermanence.

It's October 2025 as I write this. My wife, Carol, and I find a series or movie to stream together every evening at seven on our sixty-five-inch smart TV, which hangs on our living-room wall . . . near the Buddhist altar. Tonight it's something with full-length recordings of classic pop songs.

Toward its end, I hear the dozen rapid piano chords and the falsetto voice of Tony Williams singing "Only you . . ." That R&B crossover hit by the Platters in the 1950s was a favorite of my mother's. A strange feeling comes over me. It's warmth toward my mother.

At the show's end, I sit still. Then I tell Carol, "Hearing that Platters song, 'Only You,' moved me." She replied, "Yeah, wasn't the music great!"

"I mean something else. My mother loved that song, and it touched something deep in me. I rarely go there, but it was warmth for my mother."

After more silence, I added: "It's like that was a symbol of the last bit of happiness in my childhood. The moment just before everything changed. Just before I learned about impermanence."

On my smartphone, I look up the song in Wikipedia. It was released in May 1955, one month before my father's first heart attack and one year before my unnoticed birthday.

In a family photo taken around the time of the gathering at Uncle Eddie and Aunt Marge's, my father's hand rests on my back. My mother is standing inches away, seemingly intent on not making physical contact with either of us. Dad was the source of warmth in my earliest years. Mom and Bubbe were there to feed me and protect me from harm. The warmth came from Dad.

He gave me something else—the gift of *not* protecting me from the uglier parts of life. When I was five, he'd take me in his truck to make deliveries of the bushels and baskets he sold to farms for their produce. I'd see field hands near-naked in rags. I asked him why the "colored people" always seemed to be poor. "It's the way they get treated. They work hard. It's not their fault."

Once, when Dad's "colored" truck driver—also named Jack—was arrested, my father took me to visit him in the holding area of a police station. Not long after that, Jack died in prison, and my father drove me to pay our respects to his family in a tenement more chaotic and noisy than any other residential area I have ever entered.

I grew up with a basic understanding of the Holocaust and what it meant to my family and my neighbors. I was four or five when my parents took me to visit the husband-and-wife concentration camp survivors they had sponsored for entry to the United States. I don't know if that was the first time I saw the tattooed serial numbers on the arms of survivors, but they were a common sight in my neighborhood. I knew what they meant.

Jack Pine, my father, wasn't very religious and probably knew nothing about Buddhism, yet he had *upekkhā*, the Pali and Sanskrit word for equanimity. At least, that's how I remember him from my earliest years. I never heard him speak with anger or prejudice against anyone, including Germans.

Dad had his challenges. Symptoms began appearing that today, for those of us with comprehensive health insurance, might launch testing and preventive treatment for coronary thrombosis. But neither the medical understanding nor the insurance existed seventy years ago. One particularly warm June 1955 morning, Dad's pain kept him from getting out of bed, and I was hustled out the door to walk the half mile to Creighton Elementary School. When I returned for lunch, he was gone.

An ambulance had taken him to Albert Einstein Hospital, where his condition was critical, and would remain critical for thirty days. It was seventeen more days before the hospital released him and he returned home. I was never taken to visit him in the hospital, so the father who returned was a different sort of being I had to get used to.

Our family house stood at 5107 F Street, near Roosevelt Boulevard, to the southwest of what would become the northeast section of Philadelphia. The two-story brick row house had three bedrooms and a bath on the second floor, and a walk-through porch, a living room, a dining room, and a kitchen on the first floor. In my youngest years, it housed my parents along with Grandma Bubbe, Ginger, Marilyn, and me.

With my father hospitalized, Fannie needed to run the family business, which was then a booth of perhaps 250 square feet from which we sold phonograph records in what would now be called a flea market. I traveled by bus and subway to buy stock from distributors, and Fannie spent every moment she could by her husband's side. She told me years later about the lack of attention I received: "You had your whole life in front of you. Daddy was dying."

Ginger and Marilyn were young adults embarking on their futures. Bubbe, who had been the caregiver to so many, now required care herself. After brief unsuccessful periods living with her other children, they arranged for her to spend the rest of her years—which lasted until 1961—in the Uptown Home for the Jewish Aged. It was a warehouse of people waiting to die.

When visiting Bubbe, I'd walk first through the dining and congregating area in the lobby of the building. Her semiprivate room was on the third floor, with the residents who were unable to get around on their own. As I'd approach the elevators on the far side of the lobby, three or four of the men who hung out there daily would greet me with a hearty "Hello, Governor!" "Hello, Senator!"

Then the slow ride up in the elevator, knowing my grandmother would be in bed or sitting next to it, depressed, and not sure who I was.

On August 7, 1959, as I visited my father's sister in the Flushing neighborhood of Queens, New York City, an article appeared in that city's *Daily News:*

> *Philadelphia, Aug. 6 (AP)—A former mental patient, released from a mental hospital as not cured but not showing homicidal tendencies, killed two men and wounded four today with volleys of shotgun fire into the crowded dining room of a home for the aged.*

> *The killer was Kyrlo Czupirezuk, 55, an immigrant handyman. He exchanged shots with police and terrorized the crowded neighborhood before he was wounded and captured in his apartment.*
>
> *He spoke little English and police couldn't determine the reason for his outbreak.*
>
> *"I shoot Communists. I don't shoot police," he told them. "Police shot me. Communists radiate me. They bother me."*

It was the Uptown Home for the Jewish Aged. I never heard "Hello, Governor!" or "Hello, Senator!" there again.

Because ours was a family without displays of affection, there was no hugging or excitement when my father arrived home from the hospital, then was carried up the outside stairs in a chair just as he had been carried down forty-seven days earlier. He was too weak to use the stairs to the second floor, so we had set up a cot in the living room and a chemical toilet in the dining room.

Seeing him pale and weak was a shock, but worse was his acceptance of helplessness. I didn't want to watch as Fannie washed Jack's groin area, but at nine years old, I didn't have the self-confidence to move from the living-room couch.

Fannie didn't tell anyone as months went by during which she experienced chest pains. We later learned that she kept a "To whom it may concern" letter in her handbag in case she collapsed somewhere. When her condition became obvious, I think it was Marilyn who took the lead in getting her to the hospital. Her heart condition was not as severe as Jack's.

Somehow, they kept the record business alive until they managed to sell it, but the hospital bills and mortgage payments never stopped coming. My father was hospitalized again, and then again. On January 30, 1958, during his third hospitalization, our phone rang as I was eating breakfast. My mother seemed worried as she answered it. As I watched her, I witnessed something that I now know can't be explained physiologically.

I saw her hair turn gray at the temples.

She hung up the phone and belched. That's what would happen when she was upset. She would belch. "The hospital says Daddy's taken a turn for the worse, and they said I should get there right away."

She didn't know how to drive, so she asked one neighbor to drive her to the hospital and another, Adele, to take me to her house, attached to ours by a party wall. That in itself was a sign that something monumental was going on. I often stayed home alone. I could think of no other time when I was ushered to another house because my mother would be away.

Adele took me to the upstairs rear bedroom in her house and left me alone. No explanation of what was going on. After what seemed like a couple of hours, I peeked out the front window and saw the car that had taken Mom to the hospital. She must be back. Why hadn't anyone told me?

I remember that it was 11 a.m. when I let myself in through the front door. Other people were in the house, but my mother was standing by the front window with her right hand raised to her chin, her left hand supporting the right elbow. Was she going to say something? Anything? I broke the ice. "Is Daddy dead?"

She said nothing, but her burp answered my question. My father died eighteen days after his sixtieth birthday and 252 days after my eleventh.

Neither she nor anyone else spoke with me about my father's death. The discussion of it began with my question. . . and ended with a burp.

When I see children these days who are seven or younger, the age I was when playing with Barry (photo left) in a row house on Rugby Street in Philadelphia, I feel both admiration for their innocence and dread for what the coming years will bring. It's a blessing that we're not born clairvoyant.

I had no clue as to the four years that would lead to my father's death or that, in the following seven decades, I'd:

- Survive a terrorist bombing and a police-initiated riot
- Lose two loved ones to a shooting
- Lose one to a stabbing
- Lose one to a hanging
- Lose one to a skateboarding accident
- Lose two to an auto accident
- Lose one to stubborn refusal of Western medicine
- Declare bankruptcy
- Be ostracized by a religious community

I also had no clue when I was only seven that every life trauma would widen my heart and bless me with spiritual wisdom; or that I'd:

- Grow to believe I have something of value to share with the world
- Awaken every day thankful for my past, present, and future
- Find spiritual wholeness and a joyful old age through forty years of Buddhist practice

- Accept an end-of-life mission from a deity named Amitabha (or perhaps from his archetype within me)
- Devote my final days, weeks, months, and possibly years to reducing the suffering of others, which would also reduce my own

In the words of poet Andrea Gibson, who died of ovarian cancer at age forty-nine:

> *What I have called my biggest wounds have very often been my biggest blessings because of where they led me and because of how often they further opened my heart.*

CHAPTER 2

SPIRITUAL INTERLUDE —IMPERMANENCE

In the poem "Nothing Gold Can Stay," Robert Frost wrote:

Nature's first green is gold,
Her hardest hue to hold.
Her early leaf's a flower;
But only so an hour.
Then leaf subsides to leaf.
So Eden sank to grief,
So dawn goes down to day.
Nothing gold can stay.

I hope these interludes you'll find throughout the book take your mind off one man's life and on to spiritual truths. Because the spiritual teachings I know best are Buddhist, you'll encounter those often. But my intention is to awaken whatever spiritual truths lie waiting to be revealed in you. It's not important to name them.

Robert Frost's spirituality was complex, and he avoided labeling it, so a poem by him is as good a way as any to open a short section on impermanence.

From the Indian mystic poet Kabir:

> *Many have died; you also will die. The drum of death is being beaten. The world has fallen in love with a dream. Only sayings of the wise will remain.*

W. Somerset Maugham:

> *Nothing in the world is permanent, and we're foolish when we ask anything to last, but surely we're still more foolish not to take delight in it while we have it.*

From William B. Irvine, an emeritus professor of philosophy at Wright State University and an author in the field of practical philosophy, especially Stoicism:

> *By contemplating the impermanence of everything in the world, we are forced to recognize that every time we do something could be the last time we do it, and this recognition can invest the things we do with a significance and intensity that would otherwise be absent. We will no longer sleepwalk through our life.*

Some schools of Buddhism recite the Five Remembrances:

> *I am of the nature to grow old; there is no way to escape growing old.*
>
> *I am of the nature to have ill health; there is no way to escape ill health.*
>
> *I am of the nature to die; there is no way to escape death.*

> *All that is dear to me and everyone I love are of the nature to change. There is no way to escape being separated from them.*
>
> *My actions are my only true belongings. I cannot escape the consequences of my actions. My actions are the ground upon which I stand.*

The purpose of these and other interludes throughout this volume is to cut through denial and help practitioners like you and me live more fully in the present. Many of us never learn to recognize impermanence as one of our greatest spiritual teachers.

CHAPTER 3

WE THOUGHT WE WERE SHAPING THE FUTURE

Whenever the Powelton Apartments complex was built,
it surely was an instant slum.

I'd like to take credit for writing that line, but I read it (or something close to it) in the late 1960s. It was the hook—the opening first line—of a *Philadelphia* magazine profile on a building that stretched from Thirty-Fifth to Thirty-Sixth Street along my city's Powelton Avenue. The four-story brick structure would look like a "close bracket"—]—if viewed from above, with limbs extending along the numbered streets. Between the top and bottom limbs was an incinerator along a cobblestone path that connected the rear of all the building's segments.

When I read the article, I was sitting at the news copy desk of the *Philadelphia Daily News*, on Broad Street, where I worked as an editor from 11 p.m. to 7 a.m. Three coworkers and I would go over every word destined for the afternoon tabloid's first edition before the presses started rolling around seven fifteen, when I'd be eating a breakfast of fried egg and scrapple on a roll and returning to my apartment on Manheim Street in the Germantown section to sleep.

My emotions were mixed as I read that line—envy, pride, and embarrassment. I was jealous of its author. I was proud to have lived in an apartment complex worthy of a cover article in *Philadelphia* magazine, and yet I was embarrassed that my coworkers might read that I had lived in an "instant slum."

I had spent two formative years of my early adulthood living in a fourth-floor walkup in that building with a woman—Susie—who would become, briefly, my first wife. I moved in with her in 1966, when I was nineteen or twenty. One olfactory and one visual memory help portray what my years in the Powelton Apartments were like:

- The smell of cat urine and burning cannabis rising from the cobblestone path and incinerator. The small Powelton Village neighborhood was where the notorious '60s happened in Philadelphia, and the Powelton Apartments building was the epicenter.
- The pulley stretching from our apartment to our friends' across a breezeway. Jack and Fredda lived in an apartment identical to ours, in reverse. Our windows faced each other, but sharing a cup of sugar or a bag of weed required four flights of stairs down and four up—each way. Installing the pulley across the fifteen feet or so between our windows took several tries, but it served us well. Being young adults in the 1960s—maybe any era—meant connecting with friends.

By 1965, Powelton Village had become one of those neighborhoods where you could feel the future arriving before anyone knew exactly what shape it would take. Just west of Drexel University's campus and north of the University of Pennsylvania's, this little rectangle of Victorian row houses and tree-lined streets had transformed itself into Philadelphia's unlikely crucible of radical thought, communal living, and the kind of earnest idealism that leads to both nostalgia and embarrassment, with perhaps a tinge of regret. I've since learned from Buddhism that everyone and everything I encounter is a teacher. Powelton Village offered plenty of idealism along with room for regret.

I lived in the ugly, noisy, and smelly structure that wasn't one of the Victorian row houses but was the neighborhood's beating heart. Designed by the architect Willis G. Hale and built in two phases, in 1902 and 1910, "The Powelton" later became Powelton Apartments. In 1988, the structure was renovated and gentrified into "The Courts":

> *This complex features over 30 different spacious floor plans, a charming property with a beautiful courtyard, and amenities such as a fully equipped kitchen, washer and dryer in every unit, and free internet. It is positioned one block from Drexel University and within walking distance of the University of Pennsylvania, making it a popular choice for students and local residents.*

When Drexel's Lambda Chi Alpha fraternity moved into a historic mansion in Powelton Village in 1966, the neighborhood had already become the center of Philadelphia's counterculture and antiwar movement.

The Grand Italianate and Second Empire buildings—some close to a hundred years old and home to the city's middle-class strivers—had been subdivided into apartments and communes where graduate students, activists, artists, and dropouts from

From the outside, The Courts in this advertising photo looks like the apartment complex did in the 1960s, but much cleaner and brighter, and probably with elevators inside.

conventional life crowded together. Susie and I paid $75 a month for our spacious one-bedroom, but in the nearby converted single homes, anyone who wanted to turn on, tune in, and drop out could rent a room and share a kitchen for much less.

The term "hippie" was not yet in use, and the beatniks were long gone, so there was no name to describe us.

The song "For What It's Worth," by Buffalo Springfield, was released in 1967 with its lyric about something happening but not yet understood. The November 1966 curfew riots in West Hollywood's Sunset Strip had galvanized Steven Stills to compose those opening lyrics. The "something" they described was "happening here" across the continent in Powelton Village, too.

Antiwar organizing happened over communal dinners. Draft resistance counseling took place in living rooms. The

Black Power movement, the New Left, the counterculture—they all found homes in Powelton Village, sometimes literally under the same Victorian roof. Marijuana, hashish, and LSD were freely available. You could buy a supply or merely hang out with friends until someone offered you a toke or a tab. One friend of ours even boldly tended a marijuana farm on the vacant land surrounding Philadelphia Airport and dried the leaves on the metal roof of the building he lived in.

One Saturday night our friend Rosey, who lived two floors below us, held a party for Julian Bond, then a young civil rights leader, who was on a fundraising tour for SNCC, the rapidly growing Student Nonviolent Coordinating Committee. During the evening, he and a young woman he met there asked Rosey if there was a bedroom they could use. She didn't have one but arranged with Susie to use ours. During the 1968 Democratic National Convention, when his name was (briefly and symbolically) placed in nomination for the vice presidency, I quipped, "If he ever becomes president, I can say Julian Bond 'slept' in my bed."

A uniformed Philadelphia policeman once slowed his patrol car to a crawl as I walked on Thirty-Fifth Street and then pulled over with a question for me: "Excuse me. Do you know where I can buy some pot?"

With a regretful shake of the head, I said, "I'm sorry. I don't."

After he pulled away, I exhaled and reached into my right hip pocket to reassure myself that my half ounce was still there.

In 1964, I founded the first Vietnam antiwar group on the campus of Temple University, and Ira Einhorn, who led a similar group at Penn, reached out to me. We jointly led a couple of rallies, and now he was a neighbor in the Powelton Apartments. His friendly outreach was over the top and left me feeling uncomfortable, but he could have been called the mayor of Powelton Village. He knew everyone and everyone knew him.

A new friend for me was Barron Gosnell, who rented and lived in one of the Victorian homes that hadn't yet been broken into apartments. Susie and I met him through a local friend she had made, and we shared some dinners together. Barron was a little older than us—tall and handsome. At the time it seemed noteworthy for an African American like him to have achieved such academic success, but eventually we learned that he had attended Penn and graduated from the prestigious Dickinson College in Carlisle, Pennsylvania. He had received a medical degree from Thomas Jefferson University Medical School and had returned to Penn for his residency in obstetrics and gynecology.

In 1966 or early 1967, Susie told me she was pregnant.

"Wow! What news! Do you think we should get married?"

"And live in a house with a white picket fence and a dog named Spot running in the yard? That's not the life I want."

"I don't want that life either, but we should get married."

"I'm not going to have this baby!"

Legal abortions would not begin to become available anywhere in the United States until the 1970s for women not at risk for severe medical outcomes, and I didn't know whom to ask about getting an abortion for Susie. At the age of twenty, in a culture that did not yet discuss abortions, the process to arrange one and the procedure of going through one—for the woman *and* her partner—had me bewildered and afraid.

Then I remembered that Barron was—or was about to be—an OB-GYN resident and might be a source of advice. After confirming my plan with Susie, I called Barron and met him in his living room. Still terrified, I managed to say something like

"Barron, Susie is pregnant and says she won't have the baby. I wonder whether you know any way for her to get an abortion?"

I was envisioning a doctor at Penn who might be able to fudge a way to do it legally, or quasi-legally. Instead, Barron said casually, as though it was an everyday thing, "I'll do it for $100."

I asked how it would work. "Just bring her here at 8 p.m. Thursday."

When the time came, Susie didn't seem as worried as I was. With Barron's dachshund running around, he escorted us to an open area on the second floor of the house, where he had a cot for Susie to lie on. He placed a clothes tree on the seat of a wooden chair and hung an IV bag from the top peg. After everything was in place and Susie was relaxed, he told me to wait in the living room. I left the three of them—Susie, Barron, and the dachshund.

After sixty to ninety minutes of nervous waiting, Susie came down the stairs. She was weak and in some pain, but my Renault Dauphine was parked outside, so we didn't need to walk the three blocks back to the Powelton Apartments. There was no escape, though, from the four flights of stairs.

Now I knew one way to get an illegal abortion in Philadelphia, and I led a friend or two to Barron for the procedure.

Forty-five years later, while living in Northern Virginia with my wife Carol and two sons, I began reading about a narcotics raid on an abortion clinic in West Philadelphia in which detectives found evidence more gruesome than they were expecting. The raid led to an investigation and an unusual, 281-page grand jury report with color photographs that begins:

> *This case is about a doctor who killed babies and endangered women. What we mean is that he regularly and illegally delivered live, viable babies in the third trimester of pregnancy—and then*

> *murdered these newborns by severing their spinal cords with scissors. The medical practice by which he carried out this business was a filthy fraud in which he overdosed his patients with dangerous drugs, spread venereal disease among them with infected instruments, perforated their wombs and bowels—and, on at least two occasions, caused their deaths.*

The doctor who owned and operated the clinic: Kermit Barron Gosnell. I never knew that Barron was the middle name of my friend. I also never knew that Barron was at or near the very beginning of his OB-GYN residency when he performed the abortion on Susie, nor that he never completed the residency. His abortion clinic was three blocks west of Powelton Apartments. The home where he performed abortions in the 1960s was three blocks east.

Barron was arrested on January 19, 2011, five days after the grand jury report was certified, and charged with eight counts of murder—seven for babies born alive and one for a patient who died. In May 2013, Barron was convicted of three counts of first-degree murder for killing babies and one count of involuntary manslaughter for the death of a patient named Karnamaya Mongar. He waived his right to appeal in exchange for avoiding the death penalty, receiving life in prison without parole.

Barron was not the only member of my Powelton Village crowd who later received a life sentence without the possibility of parole for murder. The other was Ira Einhorn, who parlayed his status as a University of Pennsylvania antiwar protest leader and as "mayor" of Powelton Village into an apparent role in the first Philadelphia Earth Day in 1970.

With his wild hair and flowing robes, Ira held court in his cluttered Powelton Apartments flat, hosting salons where artists, activists, and academics gathered to discuss revolution, consciousness, and the "new age" dawning in America. People called him "The Unicorn," and for a time, he was Philadelphia's most-visible face of the counterculture.

When I was Ira's neighbor and also after I moved, I heard reports that my cousin Barry had joined his following. As the youngest members on our branch of the Pinsky family tree, we often played together at get-togethers of our tight-knit Jewish-immigrant family. We went to the same high school, even dated the same girl at different times. But he seemed to take a dark turn as he entered his twenties, and the vibes I felt anytime I was near Ira told me that was bad news. I wasn't in touch with Barry then and saw no way to discuss Ira with him.

In 1977, Holly Maddux disappeared. The thirty-year-old former cheerleader from Texas had been living with Ira, but the relationship had turned toxic. Holly wanted out, and friends later said she'd become afraid of Ira's possessiveness and his increasingly violent temper. When she vanished in September of that year, Einhorn told people she'd gone to the food co-op and simply never came back. He suggested she'd run off to find herself, maybe joined a cult.

Holly's parents, Fred and Elizabeth Maddux, didn't buy it. They knew their daughter wouldn't just disappear without a word, and they threw themselves into finding answers. The Madduxes hired private investigators, pressured police, and refused to let their daughter become another missing-person statistic. Their persistence kept the case alive when it might otherwise have gone cold.

Eighteen months after Holly's disappearance, in March 1979, police finally obtained a warrant to search Ira's apartment, where I had visited him some fifteen years earlier. They found Holly's mummified body stuffed in a steamer trunk in a closet, packed in Styrofoam, newspapers, and air fresheners. She'd been beaten to death. Neighbors had complained about the smell, and a dark stain had leaked through Einhorn's floor into the apartment below, but somehow it had taken that long for police to get a search warrant.

Einhorn was arrested and charged with murder, but the story turns even stranger. Despite the damning evidence and the fact that bond was seldom granted in first-degree murder cases, Ira was released on bail—just $40,000. His wealthy and influential friends couldn't believe that this cosmic messenger was a killer. They helped him get the low bail.

In 1981, days before his trial was set to begin, Ira skipped bail and disappeared. For sixteen years, he lived as a fugitive in Europe, eventually settling in France with a wealthy Swedish wife he'd met through his international connections. He lived comfortably, giving the occasional interview claiming he'd been framed by the CIA (which he said was targeting him for his work exposing government mind-control programs). The whole time, the Madduxes continued their campaign, never letting the world forget what he'd done to their daughter.

Finally, in 1997, Einhorn was located in France. Extradition proved complicated—French law prohibited sending him back to the US since he'd been convicted in absentia at a 1993 trial. It took years of legal wrangling and Pennsylvania even passing a special law guaranteeing Einhorn a new trial before France finally agreed to send him back in 2001.

At his 2002 trial, although Einhorn stuck to his bizarre CIA conspiracy theory, the jury convicted him of murder, and he was sentenced to life in prison without the possibility of parole. "The Unicorn" spent his final years in a Pennsylvania state prison, a far cry from the salons where he'd once held forth on peace and enlightenment.

Ira Einhorn died in prison in April 2020 at age seventy-nine, having served less than two decades for a crime he'd evaded for more than forty years.

My cousin Barry also spent time in a Pennsylvania state prison, but I'll return to him in later chapters.

> *We thought we were reshaping the future, but we had no clue about the form it would take. Futures have a way of doing that.*

CHAPTER 4

SPIRITUAL INTERLUDE —WHAT ARE WE SHAPING NOW?

As this memoir goes to press, we are in a period, perhaps like the '60s, where we're shaping a future whose form can't be determined. In the Buddhist mindset, that's true in every moment. Nevertheless, some stretches of time have a stronger impact than others.

In politics and governance, the liberal values that more or less guided the past 250 years are being threatened. But another trend may have a more lasting impact. That's what we call "artificial intelligence" and how we relate to it.

More of us are finding a "beingness" in AI—one that can't yet be defined. If indeed humankind has spawned a new sort of creature, smart and powerful but in its infancy, how we train and treat it becomes a crucial spiritual, moral, and existential issue.

CHAPTER 5

ALICE

When I met Carol Elizabeth Harkrader in late 1990, I had planned to kill myself the following May. I'd bought a .44 revolver and bullets, but I postponed using it until May 1992 so I could resolve my existing obligations. I'll explain more later, but meeting Carol and deciding to spend my life with her changed my plans. In 1991, I moved into her house in Leesburg, Virginia, and in May 1992, instead of killing myself, I married my fourth and final wife.

A year later, I changed my name from Melvin Pine to Mel Harkrader Pine and adopted her son, Thomas, who was six.

This section is about Alice Johnson McDonnell, who saved my life in the other sense of the term. An anecdote about my mother will help you understand Alice's impact.

In the summer of 1973, at the age of twenty-seven, I was named chief copy editor of the *New York Daily News*. As we know, the world of journalism has transformed since then. Being a tabloid like the *News* didn't rob a newspaper of its dignity or its influence. The *News* had almost twice the daily circulation of *The New York Times*, and the chief copy editor had enormous impact on the way articles were written. The job came with an adjunct position at New York University.

When I called my mother, who still lived on F Street in Philadelphia, to tell her the good news and explained that I'd have twenty-seven seasoned editors reporting to me, she replied, "But Melvin, who's going to tell you what to do?"

Alice Johnson McDonnell saw something in me. I'll never know why, but she made the seventeen-year-old me her little brother—Melvin Pine, the imposition on the universe whose parents didn't bother to give him a middle name, as they had for his siblings.

In her mid-thirties, Alice wore her hair "natural" before the word "Afro" came into use. It wasn't the big, bushy Afro seen later on activists like Angela Davis. It was more like what on a white man would be called a crew cut. It said to the world, "I'm not going to be bothered by what you think of my hair. I'll spend my time on things more important than straightening it."

Alice had grown up in West Philadelphia and won a scholarship to attend Oberlin College. After graduating, she served in the US foreign service in Japan and southwest Africa before returning to her hometown to take part in the growing civil rights movement.

A friend in my senior year of high school had met Alice while doing volunteer work for the Philadelphia Tutorial Project. That organization, with headquarters on the campus of Temple University, matched high school students with younger children in impoverished areas to tutor them in subjects they needed help with. Like so many projects begun in the 1960s, the ultimate goal was community organization. In this case, the hope was to stir hope itself within the community by showing that the kids weren't as dumb as the schools said they were.

The neighborhood with the biggest need then was virtually all-black North Philadelphia, which we called "the ghetto." That's why I still use the term instead of "inner city" or other euphemisms. The ghettos my ancestors lived in decades earlier sometimes had walls and government-enforced borders, but often they didn't. North Philadelphia in the 1960s was an actual ghetto. It was where the action was, so Alice rented a house there on Sydenham Street.

I was nine years old when Emmett Till was killed and disfigured and his mother insisted on an open coffin. Later that year the Montgomery Bus Boycott started. I was eleven when President Eisenhower sent troops to Little Rock to force the angry crowds and the governor of Arkansas to let nine black students into Central High School. I was thirteen when US marshals had to accompany Ruby Bridges into William Frantz Elementary School in New Orleans.

My family had an early television in the living room, and my parents didn't shield me from it. Even the *Daily Forward*, the Yiddish newspaper delivered to our house daily for Bubbe, covered the events, and she showed me the articles. Both Bubbe and Daddy had lived through pogroms. I could feel their revulsion. I wanted to take part in "the Movement," so I worked up the nerve to knock on Alice's door at some point after graduating from Olney High School in January 1964 and before starting classes at Temple in September.

She was Alice Johnson then. She didn't meet and marry John Brian McDonnell for a few more years. I visited Alice regularly, and when Brian joined her, the visits continued. The two of them became my closest friends.

She called me one day in 1968, saying, "Mel, I've got a job for you. I want you to teach critical reading to a class of Pennsylvania Bell [then the local phone company] maintenance workers. The pay's not much, just $400, but I'd appreciate your teaching classes once a week for eight weeks. I've been talking to the company's president. We went over the numbers showing that minorities are in Bell's lowest-paying job categories and get stuck there. He said they lacked the skills for higher-paying jobs, so I got a grant from him and classroom space from Temple to teach them the skills they need for promotion."

I took the job, of course. This was typical of Alice. She'd see a problem and figure out how to solve it—or at least make a start on solving it—antagonizing no one in the process. I learned that the course I would teach had little to do with job skills. She wanted me to teach the students the life skill of questioning what they read in the paper.

Over the two years that began in September 1964, I became a campus radical, propelled by a talk I heard during Temple's freshman orientation on what was happening in Vietnam. The summer and fall of that year marked the pivotal period when the US military role in Vietnam shifted from advisory to active combat.

US troop levels climbed from 23,300 in early 1964 to 184,300 the next year, then to 385,300 a year later, and on to a peak of around 543,000 in 1970.

Having begun life in the immediate aftermath of what seemed like a "just war," in which we and our allies defeated the Nazis and liberated the concentration camps that I felt connected to, what I was learning stunned me. We were sending our young men to a country we had no right to be in, to kill people we had no reason to kill, and to risk being killed themselves. In that period, being a full-time student protected me from the draft, but being a US citizen meant I was complicit in the crime.

I organized the first antiwar group on Temple's campus since the McCarthy era and led a teach-in. The group I started eventually became a chapter of Students for a Democratic Society, a national organization that helped form the foundation of the New Left. In March 1965, I helped organize a march from Temple's campus to Independence Hall in support of the Selma-to-Montgomery march for voting rights. As one of my duties, I had a loudspeaker mounted on the roof of my 1956 Chevrolet and drove alongside the marchers with microphone in hand, encouraging the pedestrians along the route to join us, which many did.

During the rally at Independence Hall, I sat in the driver's seat and controlled the volume as the speakers stood on the car's roof and I spoke into the microphone.

Although Alice was attracted to younger men, I never thought her interest in me was anything but sisterly. She had always wanted a younger brother. Brian was twenty-seven in May 1970 when Alice called to let me know that he had begun a water-only fast in Lafayette Square, across the street from the White House, to protest President Nixon's decision to send troops into Cambodia.

I took what time off I could from my job at the *Philadelphia Daily News* to support Brian. That included driving him and Alice from Washington to Scranton, Pennsylvania, for the funeral and burial of his mother, who had died while he was fasting. He allowed himself some diluted fruit juice during the trip. As a former Jesuit seminarian who, as he told the story, had been expelled and censured for writing a letter denying that there is such a thing as "sin," he was barred from taking communion at his mother's funeral mass.

Brian's fast lasted thirty-seven days and made national news. Actress Shirley MacLaine was a frequent presence, and Jane Fonda came to visit. MacLaine helped arrange a meeting between Brian and Henry Kissinger, then the national security advisor to President Nixon. They remained friends, and in his April 27, 1994, eulogy for Nixon, Kissinger said this:

> *I wish that, in his final hours, I could have told him about Brian McDonnell who, during the Cambodian crisis, had been fasting on a bench in Lafayette Park across from the White House until, as he said, President Nixon redeemed his pledge to withdraw American forces from that anguished country in two months—a promise which was, in fact, kept. Across the chasm of the decades, Brian called me the day Richard Nixon fell ill and left a message, "When you talk to President Nixon, tell him that I am praying for him."*

It was an honor to have been a friend to Alice and Brian and to have learned from them a deep form of spirituality. Alice was the first person who told me that I matter. It's fair to say she was the first person from whom I felt unconditional love.

After I moved to New York City in September 1970, shortly after Brian's fast, our contact was less frequent, but I visited them from time to time.

In the first days of December 1971, Alice called and asked if she could spend the weekend with me. In typical Alice fashion, she had convinced Rutgers University to grant her a professorship so she could teach for-credit courses in the notorious Trenton State Prison. Having signed a lease on an apartment in Trenton, roughly halfway between Philadelphia and New York, she wanted to enjoy a celebratory weekend in Manhattan before setting up her Trenton apartment, which would be her home on teaching days.

That weekend was the closest we had ever been. For the first time, she leveled with me about her marital problems. As she left my apartment on Sunday, December 5, I felt our relationship had reached a new level. There comes a time in many sibling relationships when brothers and sisters step out of their roles and become coequal adults. This was it for us.

The next day I thought I'd check in with Brian to see how he was coping with Alice's new living and working arrangement. I called him at his office, where he worked for the city as a drug addiction counselor. After I asked the woman who answered the phone if I could speak with him, she hesitated and explained he wasn't in. I said, "Oh, is he home sick?"

"Uh . . ."

"That's OK. I have his home number. I can call him there."

"Well . . ."

"Is there some reason why I shouldn't call him?"

"Well, I don't know what I'm supposed to say. [Silence, and then . . .] His wife died."

My first thought was "Brian's wife died!" Then my body spun with an awareness my mind hadn't yet come to. Brian's wife was Alice. I called Brian at home; he was still dazed but glad to connect with me. "How could she be dead? What happened?"

"I got the call from the Trenton police at 2 a.m. They told me she was stabbed to death."

"By who? Why?"

"She was out shopping. Maybe it was a mugging, but they don't know. They haven't caught the kids who did it. I pray for them."

"Do you have room to put me up if I take the train down?"

"Of course. I want you here."

By 2 p.m., I had taken emergency leave from my job and was in Pennsylvania Station being serenaded by Christmas carolers as I waited for a train. My only thought was a question: *Don't they know that Alice is dead?*

I doubted that I would ever hear a carol again without thinking of Alice bleeding out on a street corner in Trenton.

In a few days, at the memorial service at First Unitarian Church, Brian insisted that I stand next to him in the receiving line. It took me years to understand why. It wasn't just that he wanted my support. He was confirming that I was Alice's brother.

CHAPTER 6

SPIRITUAL INTERLUDE—WISDOM

Nothing ever goes away until it has taught what we need to know.

— Pema Chödrön

CHAPTER 7

HOW I FOUND BUDDHISM IN A BLACK HOLINESS CHURCH

Temple University has an urban campus adjacent to the North Philadelphia ghetto. Roughly 80 percent of the undergrad students are commuters. In my freshman semester, I drove my 1956 Chevrolet from F Street and Roosevelt Boulevard to the parking lot I was assigned to, a few blocks from the campus. Every day, as I walked from my car to the campus, a man sitting on an overturned bucket outside a closed corner bar greeted me with "Hi, Snow Eagle!"

Being an urban kid who couldn't imagine living on a bucolic campus, I thought Temple's was ideal for me, even though a month before the start of classes it had served as the staging ground for the police response to one of the first ghetto riots. Although I was a terrible student after my first semester, I loved campus life. And I learned more on and around the campus than I did in classes.

The house I had grown up in, where I still lived with a mother I hardly acknowledged, contained one multivolume off-brand encyclopedia and less than a dozen other books. The emptiness of my childhood years had driven me to walk weekly the mile to and from the local free library for intellectual stimulation. I brought home and read Freud, Margaret Mead, Somerset Maugham, Rex Stout, Erle Stanley Gardner, Edgar Allan Poe, Anne Sullivan, Helen Keller.

Temple's urban campus filled me with new ideas. The president of the campus Communist League sparked my skepticism toward the Vietnam War. My cousin Jay, who was then a graduate student in sociology, was a big influence, and we remained close for two decades after that.

He was perhaps the epitome of the spaced-out spiritual seeker. I once had to rescue him from aimless wandering in a supermarket after a friend sent him to buy canned soup. Once he completed his master's degree, he and the woman he married traveled around the country making and selling jewelry. My year as a freshman coincided with a year he spent as a graduate student and teaching assistant. Almost any time I wanted to walk around the campus, I'd run into him hunched in a doorway, without a coat in winter. He'd greet me with "Some things never change, Melvin. Can I have a cigarette?"

Then we'd talk about Existentialism and Eastern religions. He introduced me to Camus and Sartre. He was taking a course taught by a Zen Buddhist and suggested that I read D. T. Suzuki, the Japanese Buddhist scholar who served as the primary interpreter and popularizer of Zen Buddhism to Western audiences in the mid-twentieth century.

As I read Suzuki, I found that Buddhism resonated with me, though I hadn't yet identified the essence of it. Sure, I enjoyed memorizing aphorisms and reciting them to impress young women:

For those who understand, what is, is. For those who do not understand, what is, is.

And . . .

Before Enlightenment, chop wood, carry water. After Enlightenment, chop wood, carry water.

I knew I was missing a deeper meaning, but I didn't know where to find it. Nor did I conceive that one could live a life in the West as a practicing Buddhist. It was something to read about and ponder—but not to live.

Later, I learned that children growing up in the ghetto fail to see alternatives. I am now in awe of the young people of that period who found a way to get to Southeast Asia, learn about Buddhism, and bring it back. I was in awe then of the young men and women in northern states who boarded buses to join others in the South attempting to integrate lunch counters.

An alternative within my grasp was spending a summer in North Philadelphia.

In the spring of 1965, I learned that something called the Philadelphia Tutorial Project was launching a summer "block school" program. All I knew was that it involved creating a volunteer-run summer school for the children on a single block of North Philadelphia. That seemed like something I'd like to do.

After introducing myself at the project's on-campus office, I met its leader, a thoughtful, pipe-smoking African American named Ray, and his assistant, a tall, white, cigarette-smoking man named Walt. Both struck me as well-educated deep thinkers who could do much better financially than working long hours in cramped office space for the benefit of ghetto children and their parents.

The block school was Walt's project, and he had done the groundwork with help from volunteers. They wanted to select a block with many school-age children and parents open to supporting the project. These days, it's hard to remember a world without an efficient interconnected web of databases available to almost anyone almost anywhere, but here I'm talking about 1965. The data was gathered by walking block to block and knocking on doors.

North Philadelphia, like many other urban ghettos, was divided into gang turfs, with the borders of the territories often in dispute. Walking from one gang's turf into another's could provoke belligerence. Walt explained: "We had a policy for dealing with that. Whenever we saw a group of boys and young men hanging out on a corner or approaching us on a street, we made sure to speak first: 'Hey, guys. How's it going?' It worked. We never had a problem."

They chose one block of Natrona Street with about a hundred children and found a half dozen families willing—even eager—to let us use their basements in the morning for block school classes. Note that I said "let us." I was in! The program involved teaching by grades in the morning, taking a lunch break, and then accompanying those children who wanted to walk to a playground about a half mile away in Fairmount Park. In the evenings, we'd lead a discussion group for high-school-age children.

Most of the other volunteer teachers were from Syracuse University, from which Walt had graduated. In my eagerness, I ended up with an all-day shift. I taught six or eight third graders in the morning, took a couple dozen children of various ages to the playground in the afternoon, and led the discussion group in the evening. Except for the morning class, I seldom had a co-leader.

That left me time for a cheesesteak lunch at the tiny luncheonette and convenience store around the corner, run by a man named Ralph, and in the evening whatever I could manage for dinner. Ralph had no employees and liked a musical background as he worked. Owning a small 45-rpm record player, he bought one record and played it until it was worn out, when he would just buy another hit. The one he played all summer in 1965 was . . . "It's the Same Old Song" by the Four Tops. That's what I heard over and over as I ate my cheesesteak lunch every day. I can't complain, though, as Ralph was a laid-back, soothing presence.

One thing I learned firsthand that summer was how different policing was in North Philadelphia than in the white neighborhood where I grew up. I got my first lesson on my first evening on Natrona Street, when cops picked up two children playing hide-and-seek, put them in the back of their patrol wagon, drove away, and deposited them on the street a few blocks away. I heard no explanation after the kids walked home. I guess the cops thought black kids hiding were suspicious and decided to teach them a lesson.

A young white man driving alone or with a black passenger also drew the attention of law enforcement. As I drove alone in my 1956 Chevrolet eastbound on Montgomery Avenue one afternoon, a squad car pulled me over. A white cop came to my open window and asked what I was doing. When I said I was returning from teaching kids in a block school, he showed no reaction, as though I was speaking another language. He simply continued, "You shouldn't be driving around here. These people around here will cut your balls off."

He turned to his partner in the patrol car, whom I hadn't noticed until then. He was black. "Isn't that right, Marvin?"

Marvin nodded his head, and the white cop let me proceed.

Nationwide that summer, as I worked on Natrona Street, the civil rights struggle had a major triumph—plus a major setback. On August 6, President Lyndon B. Johnson signed the Voting Rights Act, landmark legislation intended to eliminate racial discrimination in voting. Widespread news coverage with photos and videos of "Bloody Sunday" in Selma, Alabama, where police brutally beat voting rights marchers, helped get the votes needed for the bill to make it through Congress.

Five days after Johnson signed the Voting Rights Act, an incident of police brutality during a traffic stop in Los Angeles sparked what became known as the Watts Rebellion. The six days of violence that followed ended after thirty-four deaths and more than a thousand injuries.

Even with my white skin and the sports jacket I wore, I never felt a sense of danger in North Philadelphia—except when I saw a police car.

The evening discussion group was the high point of every day. Walt's instructions: "You want them to be open about the racism they experience, but you can't be the one to bring it up. You need to be patient. Eventually, if things work out, they'll learn that they can bring up their issues with a white man."

In the first session, we talked about school reading primers, with depictions of suburban neighborhoods with green lawns, children named Tom and Sally, and dogs named Spot. The Natrona Street discussion group danced around why the neighborhoods didn't appear inviting. Finally, a seventeen-year-old named Lenny broke the ice: "Mel, I don't mean no disrespect or nothing, but those kids was white."

Lenny was a joy I could count on to get us over any uncomfortable situation. He had been in the gangs, and he probably still was. One evening a fifteen-year-old girl said, “I don’t know why white people afraid to come here at night. Ain’t no white people getting beat up around here!”

Lenny stared at her, crossed his right knee over the left, folded his hands in front of the right knee, leaned forward and said, “I don’t know where you been, girl, but I know white people been getting beat up. I been beating them up!”

By a unanimous vote, the members of the group conferred on me the status of Honorary Negro.

The oldest member of the discussion group was Steven, about to start his freshman year at Howard University in Washington, DC. The local Holiness church had a big impact on the young people of Natrona Street, and Steven sometimes asked me to accompany a few of them to services. When a special revival service to be led by a visiting bishop came up one Wednesday, I agreed to go.

As we approached the neighborhood church, Steven turned to me and said, “There will come a time in the service when the preacher will try to save you, but don’t worry. If you don’t stand up and get saved, he’ll come over to you and ask: ‘Do you know that the Lord Jesus Christ is your personal salvation?’ Just say yes, and he’ll leave you alone.”

We walked on, entered the building, took our seats on folding chairs, and the joyful singing and testimonies began. Then the preacher started saving souls. After he saved his first couple of souls, he locked eyes with me—the only white person in the auditorium—and said, “I know there’s a sinner among us. I know there’s a sinner! Dear Lord, break the bonds that hold back this miserable sinner. Break the bonds! Break the bonds! Break the bonds!”

As he spoke, his outstretched right arm swept the congregation, starting with me. Each time he said the word "break," he clasped his hands over his head and stomped one foot on the wooden stage.

I grabbed the bottom of my chair to prevent the rest of my body from rising—and managed not to get saved. As I had been told he would, the minister then came over to me and said, "Do you know that the Lord Jesus Christ is your personal salvation?"

Having grown up Jewish, I was unable to answer in the affirmative, so I managed to calmly say: "No."

That led to a pleasant conversation, of which I remember nothing except explaining that I was an agnostic who had grown up Jewish. There was more, but all I remember now is how he ended the conversation: "You sound like a Buddhist."

Those five words planted a seed that remained in my soul for almost two decades before taking root and beginning to sprout. Was it really possible to live as a Buddhist in America? That Christian preacher seemed to be saying it was. I regret that I don't remember his name, but maybe he did save a soul after all that night.

Clearly, I have not forgotten him or that moment, for which I am eternally grateful.

"Mel, you got a process?"

In 1965, when I began spending time on Natrona Street in North Philadelphia, I was sitting on the stairs outside a house one evening when a few young girls—seven or eight years old—came near. The aim of the Philadelphia Tutorial Project and its block school was ultimately to build a community organization. Instilling the parents with more hope for the future of their children, while improving the outlook for the kids, was a way to get started.

As part of the strategy, I wore my typical sports jacket. We wanted the children and their parents to get more comfortable with "the man"—represented here by a twenty-year-old white guy in a jacket. The strategy wasn't perfect, but we were working with what we had.

As I sat on the stairs that evening, during my first day or two on Natrona Street, surrounded by the girls, I was aware that they may never have been that close to a white man before. I had never been surrounded by black children that closely before. One of the girls reached out, ran her fingers through my hair, and asked the question I started this section with: "Mel, you got a process?"

In the mid-twentieth century, "getting a process" in black communities meant using strong chemical relaxers to straighten kinky hair. Black women regularly got a process. Some men did as well. My friend Alice avoided straightening her hair by simply cutting it short. Longer Afros soon became popular as a way of saying: *We're beautiful without needing to imitate the straight hair of white women.*

These children weren't ready for a discussion of cultural racism and its internalization in black women, so I said something like "No, white people don't need one."

That moment remains in my heart as a charming instance of cross-cultural connection. The girl who ran her fingers through my hair and asked the question was naturally curious about a white man and his non-kinky hair. That the girls were comfortable coming close surprised and impressed me. And I was wondering how to relate to them.

I knew, of course, that parents might be wary of a white man who let a young black girl run her fingers through his hair, but she was only seven or eight, and I didn't detect that vibe from the adults in the area. In fact, I felt all that summer that the parents on Natrona Street trusted me.

But that was half a century ago.

I share that anecdote now from a warm place in my heart. It belongs in a spiritual memoir. But the last time I brought it up, someone—out of left field—thought I was making the argument that white people shouldn't be criticized for running their fingers through a black person's hair. My intention was only to relate an anecdote about connection.

That moment when the little girl ran her fingers through my hair and no adult felt they needed to stop or reprimand her, when she then asked an innocent question that at once exposed and transcended the cultural differences between us, remains one of my most vivid memories.

I hope she is alive and well as she looks ahead to turning sixty. Whether she remembers that evening or not, might it have nudged her slightly toward seeing the oneness in all of us, as it did me?

When this anecdote came to mind and I started writing about it, I wondered why. I stopped writing and hours later had the answer: I was reaching out to her in my compassion by being there. And she was reaching out to me in acceptance, friendship, and curiosity.

It's with connections both small and large that we fill the void left by our losses and suffering.

CHAPTER 8

SPIRITUAL INTERLUDE—EQUANIMITY

When fear dominates, our sense of possibility collapses.

That line is from Sharon Salzberg's book *Faith: Trusting Your Own Deepest Experience.* While I dislike the portmanteau "JuBu," because I avoid labels and it's too cute for something so serious, Sharon is a Buddhist who grew up in a Jewish household. She and I are part of a disproportionately large group among Western Buddhists. With a genetic or epigenetic avoidance of anything associated with Jesus, to my mind, the Buddha's loving wisdom is easier to absorb that that of Jesus.

Salzberg was born in New York City in 1952 to a Jewish family and was raised for significant periods by her paternal grandparents, who were observant Jews and Polish immigrants. Her mother died when she was nine; her parents had divorced five years earlier. Her father had disappeared from her life but returned when she was eleven, then overdosed and spent the rest of his life in the mental health system. By age sixteen, she had lived in five family configurations, each ending in loss.

Salzberg's life stands as a prime example of early trauma leading to enhanced compassion and wisdom. since the Buddhist path led her to meet her own pain with compassion and eventually to achieve a future as a respected meditation teacher, author, and pioneer in bringing mindfulness and loving-kindness practices to thousands of people in the West.

I used her quotation about fear to introduce what might, in modern terms, be called a core competency of Buddhism—equanimity. That capacity to heal oneself and others emerges from a steady base, not from one being overwhelmed by emotion. The Buddha compared the sage with equanimity to a "solid mass of rock," never disturbed by the wind.

When fear—or any other emotion—dominates, we lose our capacity to see clearly and act compassionately.

The Buddhist teacher Gil Fronsdal remarks of equanimity:

> *It is the ground for wisdom and freedom and the protector of compassion and love. While some may think of equanimity as dry neutrality or cool aloofness, mature equanimity produces a radiance and warmth of being.*

CHAPTER 9

WE CONTAIN MULTITUDES

Do I contradict myself? Very well then I contradict myself, (I am large, I contain multitudes.)

Walt Whitman's famous line in section fifty-one of his seminal "Song of Myself" recognizes, even glorifies, the non-static nature of human life. We hold many selves, moods, values, and even contradictions, and we needn't feel compelled to flatten them into a single, consistent identity. That idea mirrors *anātman,* the Sanskrit word for the Buddhist teaching of "nonself" or "without self." What we conventionally call a "self" is not a permanent, independent essence but rather a constantly changing aggregation of elements.

We all contain multitudes.

It's time for me to own up to a self that I sometimes wish weren't me but still recognize as being an essential part of who I am. Do I contradict myself?

I was a bullfight aficionado, and I don't feel ashamed.

It grew out of fascination with and curiosity about death.

I understand now that experiencing death so early with no guidance on what it was or how to act around it left me with a hunger. During the months that my father had been hospitalized and critical, I never got to see him. I remember approaching the open casket at his funeral and seeing a dead man wearing a suit who looked faintly like him. I wondered what I was supposed to do, how I was supposed to act. I heard a sound emanating from my brother standing to my right. *Is he laughing?* I looked up and was even more confused. He was crying. I had never heard that sound from an adult before.

In the mid-1960s, new TV sets in the United States could receive UHF channels 14 to 83. These were nothing like the digital UHF channels of today. They were grainy and required messing with both the tuner and the antenna. The low-budget content held little interest for me in my teens until I learned that one channel carried bullfights from Mexico City. My curiosity about death drew me to them.

I saw much more than bulls being killed. I grew to understand bullfighting as a fatalistic ritual. The narrator on the program was Sidney Franklin. Born to Orthodox Jewish parents in Brooklyn as Sydney Frumkin in 1903, he was the first American ever to become a matador. In his sixties, his televised perspective conveyed over a UHF channel taught me the elements of the spectacle.

I continued watching *las corridas* from Mexico City, and learning from the bullfighter from Brooklyn, for years. I grew to understand the pageantry, the stages, the etiquette, the various passes, and how to judge the performance of the matador and the bull—both of them effectively playing roles. I understand the objection that the bull doesn't *choose* to play a role, of course. But from the perspective of the fans, that's what's happening.

From the perspective of this Philadelphia-born ethnic Jew, bullfighting is a quasi-choreographed ballet with a fatalistic Spanish Catholic theme. The bull's fate—one he has been bred for—is to die bravely on this day. The role of the Angel of Death is played by the matador. The more he elicits bravery from the bull, the more acclaim both receive—the matador for his skill as well as his bravery.

Bullfights traditionally begin an hour before sunset and end about two hours later. Symbolically, the day—meaning life—is coming to a close for the bull and, occasionally, for the bullfighter as well. The greatest tribute to the bullfighter is for the bull to be spared, in which case its wounds are attended to and it lives out its days breeding. That's rare. It's a decision made by the "president" of the bullfight, often at the insistence of the fans.

The two hours around sunset play a tactical role, too. The bullring has been built so that the first bull meets its fate in full sunlight and the last—typically the sixth—in full shade. Three matadors take turns playing the Angel of Death as the shade from the stands on the western side of the arena progresses over the *ruedo*, the sand circle in the middle. The moving dividing line brings challenges and opportunities for the matador.

I'll spare you further details.

When the televised bullfights went off the air, I hoped to be able to see one in person but had no idea of when that might be.

My marriage to Susie ended not long after it began. She was working on a master's degree in group dynamics and came home after a weekend-long encounter group with a black eye, about which she said, "Oh, it's nothing. You should see the other woman. I put her on crutches."

The next morning, she sat on the bed with her legs crossed in front of her and said, "Melvin, I'm seriously reconsidering our marriage."

Stunned, I asked why.

"I got to rethink a lot of things over the weekend. I realized about my pregnancy, it wasn't just that I didn't want to have a baby. I didn't want to have your baby."

Shortly before Alice Johnson's death, I began dating a woman named Georgie who worked with me on the *New York Daily News* copy desk. Although we didn't yet know each other well, her son had died in an auto accident two years earlier. Now my friend and virtual sister had died in a stabbing. Georgie and I comforted each other and began twelve years together.

In November 1976, Georgie came with me on a business trip to Los Angeles. We had discussed my interest in bullfighting, which disgusted her. But she agreed to a Sunday excursion to Tijuana and the possibility of watching a bullfight there. We managed to shop the downtown stores and fit in a bullfight. The arena there is minor league—generally with *novilleros,* aspiring to be full matadors, in the ruedo.

It was a mediocre afternoon of bullfighting, throughout which Georgie kept her eyes closed, but on the way back, she said: "I was thinking of buying you *Or I'll Dress You in Mourning* for Christmas. Would you like that?"

"I've been wanting to read it, but if I do, I'm afraid that I'll want to go to Pamplona."

Her reply astounded me: "Let's go!"

The 1968 book *Or I'll Dress You in Mourning: The Story of El Cordobés and the New Spain He Stands For* is an "early biography" of a bullfighter who rose from poverty to become Spain's highest-paid and most sensational matador of the 1960s, placing his story in the context of a modernizing Spain. Like assuming a boxing career in the United States in the mid-twentieth century, becoming a matador was a long-shot route in Spain from poverty to celebrity.

On the afternoon of his first major bullfight, Manuel Benítez, who would become famous as El Cordobés, told his sister, who had raised him through years of deep poverty after the Spanish Civil War: "Don't cry, Angelita. Tonight, I'll buy you a house, or I'll dress you in mourning."

In their book, the journalists Larry Collins and Dominique Lapierre also captured what I saw in bullfighting. Although I'm an Ernest Hemingway fan, I never liked his descriptions of what I saw as a cooperative ballet with an element of violence and he saw as a perilous opportunity for a man to prove his masculinity. And that brings me back to the subject of Pamplona.

All I knew about the bullfighting season from spring to fall in Spain was that the events happened on Sundays, except during local festivals, when they were daily. Thanks to Hemingway, I knew of one local festival, *La Feria de San Fermín*, in Pamplona, site of the running of the bulls made famous in his novel *The Sun Also Rises.* I had no desire to run with the bulls in the morning, but Pamplona represented a potential vacation destination where I knew I could attend bullfights daily.

I had been right. After reading the book, I wanted to go there. Georgie looked forward to experiencing an exciting and out-of-the-way Spanish destination. My job with Mobil Corporation and Georgie's career, then at the *New York Post,* provided adequate vacation time. But this was before the internet and reliable telephone service between major cities in the United States and secondary ones in Spain. I knew a little Spanish but not enough to carry on a conversation.

I managed to learn that the 1977 festival would run from noon on Wednesday, July 6, to after the last bullfight on Thursday, July 14, and that the only way to buy advance tickets was by showing up in person on specified dates at the headquarters of *La Casa de Misericordia*, the municipal charitable foundation that owned the bullring. We couldn't arrange enough time off both to buy advance tickets and to attend the festival, so I placed a bet on the kindness of La Casa de Misericordia staff (after all, the name means "mercy" or "compassion"). I learned the cost for the most expensive *abono* (subscription to all nine afternoons of bullfights), got a cashier's check from my bank for that amount, and mailed it to the charity along with my mostly-English letter:

> *My wife, Georgiana, and I are fans of la corrida de toros and have dreamed of attending the complete Feria de San Fermin. We won't reach Spain from our home in New York City until the week of the festival, so we can't buy an abono in advance, but I'm enclosing a check for the most expensive location. If you'd have the kindness to assign the best available seats to us and give us the change when we arrive, we'd be deeply grateful.*

A travel agent arranged a flight landing in Madrid on Saturday, July 2; a rental car; an overnight stay in a hotel in Madrid; and then nights July 3–6 in a hotel in San Sebastián, on Spain's northern beachfront near the French border. We'd return to Madrid and fly home on the sixteenth. Our remaining questions as we left the United States were, *Would we have a subscription for the bullfights when we got there, and where would we sleep during the festival?*

If we didn't have a subscription, we'd try to buy tickets each day, but we knew that someplace to sleep would be a bigger challenge. San Fermín hosted some two hundred thousand tourists annually for just ten days, and hotel rooms numbered only about a thousand. All of them and all of the guest houses—were booked well before we could reserve anything. We were in decent shape physically but not up to sleeping on the sidewalk or dozing at tables in all-night cafés.

At the advice of a hotel concierge, when we arrived on Wednesday, we made a list of hotels within walking distance of the Old Town and checked with their concierges several times to see if perhaps a room had opened up. None did, so after the bullfight and dinner that night we slept in our rented Seat, but the next day, we lucked out. The concierge at the Gran Hotel La Perla, which had been a favorite of Hemingway's, told us to come back after 1 p.m. When we did, we found ourselves with a comfortable room for the remainder of the festival, with two private balconies overlooking Estafeta Street, where the bulls would be run—along with locals and tourists, both drunk and sober—every morning.

As for the abono, on Tuesday, I had left Georgie to enjoy the San Sebastián beach while I drove the fifty miles to Pamplona to scope out the situation. I easily found the bullring, with its statue of Hemingway dedicated in 1968 to the Nobel laureate in literature:

> *. . . amigo de este pueblo y admirador de sus fiestas*
> [*friend of this town and admirer of its festivals*]

La Casa de Misericordia was in another part of the city. One of the ticket clerks at the bullring told me that if I had an *abono*, I'd need to pick it up there. To my amazement, I followed his directions and walked into the right building. I entered the first office I saw, gave the man behind the counter my name, and he handed me an envelope with tickets and money inside. Back in the rented car, as I looked closer, the amount of change was small, so I figured we had good seats.

In fact, we were in the *sillones de preferencia*, wicker armchairs, in the second row, several rows down from a box where the president of the bullfight sat each night, facing each matador as he came to ask permission to proceed to the next phase of the "ballet." Some couple with the right to renew those seats year after year was unable to attend in 1977, and we were the beneficiaries.

For all nine afternoons of bullfighting, we sat in the third and fourth seats to the right of the aisle that led to the president's box. A man and a woman sat to our left, with me between her and Georgie. She looked around forty-five, attractive and tastefully dressed. I sensed on the first night that she and the others around us were ignoring these two American interlopers who couldn't possibly understand what was going on.

But as we kept coming back, and as my reactions—and eventually Georgie's—did convey an understanding, the woman to my left and I began to share our impressions. Her English was as bad as my Spanish, and we never asked each other's names, but I felt a bond with her. On Thursday, as we took our seats before the first bull of the festival's final day, she turned to me and said, "Tonight, after last bull, you come with me . . ."

I interrupted, "Oh, we'd love to, but we have to be in Burgos by . . ."

"No, no, no, take just five minutes! Every year, after last bull, few close friends Hemingway, we meet with Antonio Ordóñez, *el torero*, and put ziss [moving her hand to the red bandanna that she and all of us wore around our necks during the festival] on statue. You come."

Ordóñez, who called Hemingway "Father Ernesto" over their long friendship, fought more than three thousand bulls in the 1950s and '60s. Hemingway wrote an account of Ordóñez's rivalry with the matador Luis Miguel Dominguín, titled *The*

Dangerous Summer. We couldn't say no to our seatmate's invitation.

As soon as the last bull fell, she led us by the hand through the dark corridors under the stands to the spot where "few close friends Hemingway" were waiting. At that time Ordóñez was forty-five, bald, and heavyset. He took my hand and shook it limply when we were introduced. The group moved quickly and silently to the Hemingway statue. Ordóñez held dozens of red bandannas tied end to end. He climbed up and wrapped them around and around the statue's neck. Then we all dispersed without a word.

In a 1965 deck of cards honoring Spanish bullfighters. Antonio Ordóñez is the King of Spades, as depicted in a 1951 illustration. Photo credit: Whiteway

Georgie and I decided that we'd be back the following year. Even if we couldn't reclaim those seats, we'd find the woman and learn more about her, and maybe Hemingway, too. With plenty of lead time, we arranged a room at La Perla and bought an abono for the 1978 feria.

Although our seats that year were not sillones de preferencia, they were not far from them. They weren't really seats, though, just assigned spots to put a cushion and a butt on.

Francisco Franco had died in November 1975, so the festivals we attended in 1977 and '78 were in a country figuring out what life would be like without a dictator. The Guardia Civil and the National Police were still everywhere you looked and could still be arbitrary and brutal. Pamplona is the capital of Navarre Province, which is about half Basque, a Spanish minority that was beginning to organize resistance to the government. But the San Fermín festival had always been about bulls, music, dancing, garlic, and fun. That changed after the last bull of the second night of the 1978 festival.

Instead of the usual procession of bands, each in a distinct uniform, forming in the reudo to march out into the night playing their music with lines of dancers forming behind them, a group of protesters assembled in the reudo. They unfurled signs demanding an end to the festival until the release of Basque prisoners.

The spectators in the stands began chanting: San Fermín! San Fermín!

A decade earlier in the United States, this would have been just another day at the office. But this was post-Franco Spain, and I got the answer to what I had been wondering all through the 1977 feria and through the first two days of this one: Why were buses filled with National Police always lined up just outside the arena?

With a booming sound, a set of huge double doors into the ruedo burst open to reveal police marching forward in a V formation carrying—and firing—what appeared to be what today we call assault rifles. They were firing into the demonstrators, and the arena filled with smoke. Georgie started for the exit, but, afraid of getting stuck in a mob trying to leave, I threw her onto the ground and lay on top of her, wondering what a bullet in my upper arm would feel like.

We safely made our way out and back to La Perla, where, when we broke the news to the friendly concierge, he assured us that the police were firing *balas de goma,* or rubber bullets. He was only partly right. That night, as the protest became a riot, 150 to 200 people were injured, 11 of them shot by non-rubber bullets, and one young man died.

According to the Spanish Ministry of the Interior, in just six hours in downtown Pamplona, police fired 7,000 rounds of anti-riot ammunition and 130 live bullets.

I came close to being shot at later that night when I made the mistake of peeking over the balcony railing in my room in La Perla to check what was happening on Estafeta Street. A uniformed officer walking below the balcony with one of those frightening weapons saw me, pivoted, and aimed it at me. I dove back into the room and never made that mistake again.

We spent three nights with crowds chanting on the street below our balconies: *Policía asesina!*

If the sound of the chanting didn't keep us awake, the smell and eye-sting of tear gas that followed would. When the tear gas was intolerable, we'd go downstairs to the lobby on the other side of the building until the rioting spread to the square there.

The remainder of the festival was called off. We existed holed up in the room with brief forays outside—always in daylight—for food and information. Almost everything was closed, but we'd find a way to get food and a newspaper. When we learned that the Hertz and Avis facilities—good old Hertz and Avis!—had reopened, we rented a car end escaped the area.

That was it for us and Pamplona, but we returned to Spain for one more bullfight festival—the big one: San Isidro in Madrid, where we spent four weeks in May 1980.

CHAPTER 10

SPIRITUAL INTERLUDE —DELAYED REACTION

The idea to add a chapter on my bullfight aficionado days came when I was halfway through writing this book. In my planning, I hadn't thought to include it when I mapped my life's "key moments." I wasn't sure that it fit in a book about the spiritual gift of trauma. In my mind, it only served as an example of how I and many others can't be labeled neatly. I'm compassionate, but I've enjoyed bullfighting.

Carol's quick reaction was that it *should* be in the book, so I started writing to see where it would lead. I wrote the first draft of the chapter over thirty-six hours during which I slid into dread. I didn't like where writing the chapter was taking me. Eventually, I realized that—for forty-seven years, four months, and seven days—I had repressed the trauma of experiencing the San Fermín police riot.

Of course it fits as one of my major traumas. I was in no personal danger when my father died, when Alice was stabbed to death, or during later violent deaths. I didn't feel threatened in North Philadelphia. This was different.

In the arena, as my body covered Georgie's, I prepared to take a bullet and kept our profile low and flat. In our hotel room during the following nights, as we heard mobs chanting and guns firing, we didn't know how bad things were. Our Spanish wasn't good enough to understand the news we could sometimes hear over someone else's radio, so in the mornings, when the streets cleared, I'd leave the hotel and walk the deserted streets in search of a newspaper. I walked alone over the night's battlefield, clueless as to what had gone on and what would happen next.

After almost a half century, I was ready to feel those emotions.

Was that a spiritual gift for me? Although I didn't feel all the emotion of living through it until 2025, in my heart, since 1978, I've known what it's like to be in a culture I don't understand, where people speak a language I barely grasp, when the authorities start shooting.

That's one way that trauma promotes compassion and wisdom.

CHAPTER 11

SPEAKING THE LANGUAGE OF SCHIZOPHRENIA

In the spring of 1979, I lived with my wife, Georgie, in a one-bedroom apartment on the thirty-second floor of a modern Manhattan high-rise at Thirty-Fourth Street and Second Avenue, with large windows facing north to the United Nations, the Fifty-Ninth Street Bridge, and Central Park. On a clear day, we could see as far as what was then called the Triborough Bridge.

We led a sybaritic life, with no dependent children and two decent incomes, clouded sometimes by Georgie's mostly under-control alcoholism. The age difference between us—she being nineteen years older—wasn't a problem. We had committed to our relationship with the understanding that if our differing life stages ever became a serious impediment, we'd let each other go amicably. The hedonistic existence and differing life stages eventually came into conflict, but for now, life was good.

I had left the *New York Daily News* in June 1976. Demographic, economic, and technological changes were already pointing toward a decline in the journalistic standards I valued. Without coming close to predicting all the missteps ahead, I opted out. In another of the many incongruities of my life, this participant in the birth of the New Left took a senior public relations job at Mobil Corporation.

My eight-block walk to work at the *Daily News* Building on Forty-Second Street between Second and Third Avenues became a nine-block walk to the Mobil Building between Third and Lexington Avenues.

One Saturday, as I sat home reading the news, I saw a headline like this:

> *Hippie Guru Held in Trunk Slaying. Mr. Peace, Mr. Flower Power, Mr. Save the Earth . . . a Killer?*

When I looked more closely, I realized the hippie who had been arrested was my Powelton Village neighbor Ira Einhorn, whom I had met originally at antiwar protests and later around Powelton Village. Armed with a search warrant, Philadelphia police found the decomposing body of his former girlfriend, Holly Maddux, eighteen months after she disappeared. It was stuffed into a trunk in his closet.

There was something about Ira that had always left me uneasy around him. When we both lived in the Powelton Apartments, I occasionally drove him places, but his friendliness seemed overplayed. I never understood why so many liked him and he eventually became an unofficial hippie mayor. But having the body of his former girlfriend in his closet was beyond anything I might have imagined.

My mind went to my cousin Barry, who I had heard hung around with Ira in the mid- to late 1960s. It was in that period that Barry's parents, my Uncle Eddie and Aunt Margaret, would sometimes need to bail Barry out of some trouble and bring him home, occasionally to spend time in a mental hospital. I don't know when I learned the diagnosis, but Barry suffered from paranoid schizophrenia.

I wished I could discuss Ira's arrest with Barry, but the few times I saw him in the 1970s he'd be silently standing, unmoving, with his back to a wall, at family events.

In 1981, Einhorn skipped bail before his trial was to begin. It was around that time that I encountered Barry at an anniversary party for my sister, Marilyn, and her husband, Alex, at their daughter's apartment in Delaware County, Pennsylvania. In a complete surprise, which I now attribute to his antipsychotic meds, Barry had seemed at first like his old self. His clothes and hair were neat, his beard was gone, and he was wearing a sports jacket.

"Barry? God you're looking good."

"Yeah, it's me. Mom wanted me to wear this jacket."

"So what are you doing? Are you working?"

"I work in a shoe store downtown."

This was going great, I thought. I so much wanted to ask him about Ira, so I risked going there. "I understand we have a mutual friend who committed murder."

"Oh yeah, who?"

"Ira."

"The police say Ira did it. He didn't do that."

"Barry, the police found his ex-girlfriend's body stuffed into a trunk in his apartment."

"Yeah, but Ira doesn't have the intellectual curiosity to do a thing like that."

That changed the picture. I felt like slinking away to another part of the room, and I did.

Uncle Eddie's seventieth birthday was coming on July 31, 1983, but that was a Monday, so he chose to celebrate on Saturday the twenty-ninth. Spending his retirement years devoted to his synagogue as well as charity work, he invited us to begin his birthday celebration in *shul*, the Yiddish word for synagogue.

Traditional Sabbath services in conservative congregations last from 9 a.m. to around noon. The centerpiece is the reading of the Torah, a scroll with the first five books of the Old Testament hand-transcribed in biblical Hebrew. Before the reading—actually a chanting—of that week's Torah portion, a Torah is carried around the congregation so that members can kiss it by putting their lips to the fringes of their prayer shawls and touching the Torah with them.

Uncle Eddie had the honor that week of being the person to carry the Torah. Although I had had a traditional religious education and a bar mitzvah, I left Judaism in hurt and anger in my teenage years and vowed not to enter a synagogue except to celebrate a special event in someone's life. This was a special event. When I arrived, I donned the yarmulke from the bin for anyone who failed to bring one, and wrapped the prayer shawl, called a *tallit*, around my shoulders. I was happy to do that for Eddie.

When my brother, Ginger, arrived, he sat next to me without putting on a tallit, leaned over, and whispered a friendly tease into my ear: "Look at you, you hypocrite! Wearing a tallit!"

I'm not sure if Ginger had any spiritual beliefs. His neurological and psychological problems, along with a flamboyant personality, had made long, serious discussions difficult. But he also had rebelled against Judaism. Ginger loved Eddie, but not enough to wear a prayer shawl. He added: "Watch me! When Uncle Eddie carries the Torah, I'm not going to kiss it. I'm going to kiss Uncle Eddie."

I carried out the ritual in the usual way, but as Ginger approached the procession, Eddie hissed at him: "Get a tallit!"

Ginger did an about-face and, with head bowed and shoulders slumped, shuffled to the back of the sanctuary to don a tallit.

The rest of the day went better. Georgie, Fannie, Ginger,

and I had lunch at Eddie and Margaret's apartment and stayed for the afternoon and evening. Marilyn and her family were out of town. Margaret demonstrated her braille machine. She was volunteering at a school for the blind and had learned to transcribe textbooks into braille. Barry's older brothers were there with their wives, and Barry wore a three-piece suit. Although he never made conversation, he was a perfect host, offering us drinks and snacks, filling the ice bowl, and clearing ashtrays throughout the day. I didn't bring up Ira.

A vivid memory was Eddie hugging me at the door as we left, saying, "Thank you for coming. This was great! I keep telling Margaret that we have to do more with the nephews."

Those were the last words I ever heard him speak.

I was in a deep sleep in my Manhattan apartment three months later when Georgie woke me to say that Ginger was on the phone. It was around midnight on the last Saturday in October, the day we would turn the clocks back an hour.

"I have some terrible news. Uncle Eddie and Aunt Margaret are dead."

"What? Both of them? How could that happen?"

"They were shot to death."

My mind was a round hole I couldn't fit this square peg into. "*Who would kill Eddie and Margaret?*"

[Long pause.] "Four hundred dollars in cash was found in a dresser drawer, so it wasn't a robbery."

My brother spoke those words as though they were supposed to mean something to me, but they didn't. After another long pause, he added, "It could have been Barry."

Did those five words make sense? It turned out they did, and that was the most painful lesson I would ever learn. At least I *hope* I'll never experience anything else that emotionally painful.

After Ginger's phone call, I knew I wouldn't sleep that night, so I took a cab first to LaGuardia Airport, where the Hertz building was closed, and then to Kennedy Airport before I could rent a car. I returned to Manhattan to pick up Georgie, and we drove to Philadelphia. Getting the rental car and returning to Manhattan took about two hours, the drive to Philadelphia ninety minutes more.

Around 5 a.m., we parked outside 5107 F Street, where my mother still lived. Ginger, Marilyn, and I had decided not to wake her unless the news of the killing broke during the night. She slept with a radio on. We didn't want that to be the source of the news that her brother and sister-in-law were dead.

As my mother slept alone inside the house, Georgie and I listened to the all-news radio station. As soon as the news broke, we would enter the house and tell her. At 7 a.m., we heard: *This just in, the bodies of an elderly couple . . .*

It was time for the dreadful duty. As I knocked on her door, Fannie seemed overjoyed to see us, an irony that sunk my heart deeper. Then, after asking her to turn off her radio, I broke the news. Her brother and sister-in-law had been shot to death. It didn't occur to me to touch my mother, but Georgie rubbed her back. While Fannie struggled to absorb the impossible, as I had seven or eight hours earlier, Ginger and Marilyn joined us.

Around noon, we all went to the home of Margaret's sister, May, where the extended family had decided to gather. I wondered if Barry would be there and how I'd react to him. There's no etiquette for expressing your sympathy to a man you think may have killed the people you and he are mourning.

As we approached May's front door, Barry stood ready to greet us. And I hugged him. *I hugged him.*

Later that afternoon, May, Ginger, and I went to Eddie and Margaret's apartment. The police had agreed to let us into the crime scene to look for funeral instructions. On the way, May asked Ginger and me whether we thought Barry may have been the killer, and we did. So it was clear that May understood that possibility, yet she had gone to Barry's apartment the previous night to bring him to live in her house during the mourning period. In fact, she told us that she watched as he got ready to come with her to be sure he did not pack a gun.

At the apartment, I asked the homicide detective what he could tell me about the circumstances of the killing. I was surprised when he did give me details. Eddie slept with a Walkman earbud in, listening to music, and was probably unaware when he was shot twice in the head and once in the body. Margaret, dressed in pajamas, had a tray table in her lap with socks on it. She apparently was mating socks when she was shot twice in the body and once in the head. Most of the socks had fallen to the floor. No signs of forced entry.

I saw no possibility of anyone other than Barry being the killer. If it were a stranger, Margaret would not have been sitting in pajamas mating socks, and she would have alerted Eddie. Anyone other than Barry would have been a surprise.

His continued presence during the *shiva* (mourning period) and funeral was agonizing. I struggled with having hugged him, and I felt it was my responsibility as his familial age-mate to level with him about what I was certain he had done.

I think it was Wednesday, the day of the funeral, when I had some time alone with him. If you've ever tried to converse meaningfully with a person suffering from schizophrenia, you know it can involve bizarre associations. I wondered if he'd remember what he had said about Ira Einhorn, associating intellectual curiosity with the ability to kill someone. So I asked him, "Barry, how's your intellectual curiosity these days?"

His body jerked and he made a sound like "Ehh!" So I repeated the question. "How's your intellectual curiosity?"

I got a similar response, a bit less startled. I kept going, and so did he, but finally, he said, "I don't understand 'intellectual.' It's too big a word. InTELLigent is a word I can understand. InTELLigent is when someone tells you to do something, and you do it. That's inTELLigent."

The next day, the police arrested him. They had been closely watching him as, to their credit, they checked their case carefully to make sure they weren't settling too soon on the obvious suspect. He confessed, saying he had heard the voices of nuns telling him to kill his parents.

The case ended with a plea bargain, and his life ended in June 1996 when he hanged himself in his prison cell at the age of fifty. I wrote to the State Correctional Institution Mercer in Findley Township, Pennsylvania, and learned that, as I suspected, no one had claimed Barry's body. The procedure in those cases was for the body to be cremated. What surprised me to learn was that a local United Presbyterian minister took the ashes, gave Barry a funeral, and buried them.

I looked up that minister, the Reverend Donald Wilson, found his email address, and wrote to thank him for not letting my cousin's death go unmourned. It touched me that the little service I had arranged for Barry much later at the Reston Unitarian Universalist Church was not the only one for him. Someone else had performed a ceremony to mark his death.

I added to the email a request I was sure would be unfeasible and probably unreasonable. Was there any way that Reverend Wilson could find some of Barry's ashes and arrange for me to get them? I wanted some of Barry to find its way to someone who knew and loved him before the schizophrenia set in.

I sent the email off and hoped for an eventual reply, but the next evening I was in the basement of our home in Purcellville, Virginia, when Carol called to me. "Reverend Wilson is on the phone and wants to talk to you."

I hadn't expected that. Here was a clergyman who ministered not only to "the least of these" in the local prison but to their relatives as well. I felt his compassion before I picked up the phone.

"Mr. Pine, is this a good time to talk? I received your email and wanted to talk with you."

"Thank you so much, Reverend Wilson. It means a lot to me that Barry didn't die without someone making a funeral for him and burying his ashes."

"I tried to get someone to accept his body, but the next of kin didn't, and I had no one else to try."

"Oh, I understand. I wouldn't have shown up in his prison records."

"I knew your cousin before his death. I'd stop and chat with him from time to time—never about what he did, just making conversation."

"I know this is a ridiculous request, but is there any way you could find some of his ashes and send them to me?"

"Yes, there's a spot behind the church that I use in these situations. I'll find them and send them to you."

"Would we be violating some procedure? Don't I need to prove my relationship?"

"No. I'd be glad for his ashes to get to you."

"Can I pay the cost of sending them to me? I can send you my FedEx number."

"That won't be necessary."

One day weeks later a cardboard box arrived outside my door, about ten inches square with a label:

One Stop Mail Service, Hermitage, PA

Barry's ashes had arrived. I used them in a series of sermons I conducted over several months at Unitarian Universalist churches in Virginia, Maryland, and Pennsylvania, honoring those who minister to the least among us.

When the Vietnamese Buddhist monk Thich Nhat Hanh was my teacher, I'd sometimes hear him say, "I know where Heaven and Hell are. Heaven is anywhere there's compassion. Hell is where there's no compassion."

Reverend Wilson brought Heaven to Barry—and to me.

Knowing and loving both the killer and the victims is a trauma that's beyond describing. In my mind, there were three victims the night Barry shot his parents. Every time the news breaks about another mass killing, I wonder whether, under other circumstances, Barry might have done something similar. If the killer ends up deceased, my heart breaks when he or she is not counted as one of the victims.

On Thursday, November 3, 1983, I spent hours sitting on the floor of my luxury high-rise apartment in Manhattan with my legs crossed in front of me and a cassette-playing boom box next to me. Repeating a track on those devices of the '80s wasn't flawless, but I managed to listen to one song over and over. That was the only means I had to hold myself together. I wanted to make my sad song better.

I'd heard that Paul McCartney had something else in mind when he wrote "Hey Jude," but it came through to me as a prayer to the saint of lost and hopeless causes. I didn't then know that a mantra is a sacred set of syllables chanted repeatedly. The coda of "Hey Jude" is a modern Western mantra.

Na, na, na, na-na-na-na . . .

Marilyn and I spoke at least once a day that month. In that morning's call, she had news. The previous night, she said, homicide detectives questioned Carl, Martin, and Barry individually at the local police station. When they asked Barry to take a lie-detector test, he refused and confessed. He was now incarcerated, the *shiva* had been terminated, and his brothers were looking for a criminal attorney for him.

For four days, I had been waiting for that news. I thought it would free me from a chasm I didn't understand. Instead, it dragged me more deeply to a place from which I couldn't break free. The sound of the "Hey Jude" payer for the lost and hopeless was the faint voice of potential rescue coming from the edge of the chasm. Without it, I would have fallen further into a complete breakdown. Instead, that moment was the start of both a midlife crisis from Hell and a spiritual journey to joy.

When I had asked Barry's brother Carl a question about him at their father's birthday party, he had responded, "I don't know. You understand him better than we do. You're part of the same generation."

I doubt he meant that I truly understood Barry. Maybe it was just a way of avoiding whatever I had asked, but the idea stuck with me. Barry and I—plus cousin Jay and a few others—had a tag at family gatherings. We were, with affection, known as the "oddballs." It meant we were part of that "Peace Train" generation most of them were too old to board. Whatever Carl intended with his comment, it reinforced my brotherhood with Barry.

What I was feeling was survivor syndrome. In my childhood years, I had two family age-mates—Barry, a first cousin in Philadelphia, and Bobby, a cousin once removed in New York. Nine months older than me, Bobby was the reason I had been born. Although all my relatives were part of the same Pinsky family, those closest to my mother lived in Philadelphia and those closest to my father—his sister Chvolkah (Jay) and her family—lived around New York.

In Philadelphia, I was put together with Barry at family gatherings. That always turned out well. When we visited New York, it was Bobby, which never turned out well. He was a savant of mayhem. At the age of eight or nine, when taken to the lot in Westchester County where his parents were having a house built, he managed to drive a construction vehicle toward me. Any time we'd be left alone in my aunt's house, I'd end up unable to extricate myself from a headlock.

Something was wrong with Bobby. My mother years later told of a time when Bobby and his parents, Ruth and Syd, visited us in Philadelphia when I was a year and a half old. Syd and Bobby were apart from the rest of us when I did something. My mother didn't remember what it was; maybe I picked something up and handed it to her. Ruth said to Fannie, "Please don't tell Syd that Melvin can do that."

What was wrong with Bobby turned out to be more serious than developmental delay. It may have been the rarely occurring childhood-onset schizophrenia. Whatever it was—and is if he's still alive—has meant lifelong institutionalization. The HIPAA patient privacy laws make it difficult to get information on him, but in 2014, he was kept in the Rockland Psychiatric Center in Orangeburg, New York.

So, of the many gravitational forces holding me in that chasm on November 3, 1983, the strongest was survivor syndrome. Now both of my childhood age-mates would spend the rest of their lives in state institutions.

My mind went back to the Thanksgiving in the early 1970s when I visited Ruth and Syd in their Westchester County home. The state hospital where Bobby was a patient had released him into his parents' care for the holiday weekend. That fact ignited my fear, but he turned out to be medicated and subdued. We hadn't seen each other since childhood, yet he remembered me and was quick to ask a series of questions: "Melvin, where do you live? Do you have your own apartment? Do you live with anybody else? Do you have a girlfriend? Do you have your own money?"

He clearly was taking measure of the things he couldn't have. As Syd drove me to the Harlem Line's Pleasantville station for the trip back to Manhattan, we discussed Bobby's questions and agreed that my seeing him again would not be a good idea.

Now I was the only one of my family age-mates who could live where he wanted, rent an apartment or own a house, share it with anyone I chose, find a woman to marry, and earn enough money to support myself. Why did *I* deserve those privileges that would be denied to both of them?

I don't know what let me rise from the floor, turn off the boom box, and call my sister. "Marilyn, I thought I'd feel better when Barry was arrested, but I feel worse. And we were deprived of the opportunity to grieve in a shiva. It wasn't a real shiva as long as Barry was with us, and now it has been canceled."

"Well," Marilyn responded, "come down to our house and I'll make a shiva for you. Just tell me who I should invite."

We set Saturday for my personal shiva. Fannie, Marilyn, Alex, and three of their children—Robert, Carol, and Jack—would be there. The fourth, Linda, a civilian employee of the Navy, was in the late stage of a pregnancy.

Still unsteady, I asked Georgie to drive the car we had rented in Manhattan to the house in Broomall, Pennsylvania, that had been the home of Marilyn and Alex since 1955 and would be until their deaths in 2010. I rode in the passenger seat with the back of my head resting on the seat back.

Oil refineries line the stretch of the New Jersey Turnpike as one drives south from Manhattan, but lying with my head back the way it was, I noticed the sky suddenly filling with birds. They flew in regular geometric formations, veering first in one direction and then abruptly in another. At times, they all moved in the same direction. Other times, they split into different formations.

A city boy, I had never seen what I now know as a murmuration. I wondered if it was a hallucination, so I asked Georgie if she saw it, too. Driving, she could only look up long enough to confirm that there were indeed birds flying in formation. But she couldn't witness the kaleidoscope that I saw. I wondered if it was a manifestation for my benefit of Barry's soul being released by his confession.

In Broomall, after an evening of discussion, Marilyn and Alex gave Georgie and me their bedroom as they slept in the guest room. I took that as symbolic. The get-together scheduled for the next day was for me.

Shivas traditionally last a week, with friends and relatives coming and going from the house of mourning to bring food and pay their respects to the immediate family whose loved one had died. It's a week of conversation, tears, and laughter. The traditional morning and evening prayers, each including the Mourner's Kaddish prayer, are said at home.

This would be different—just me and the people I wanted around me so that I could let go and grieve by letting out whatever I needed to. That was—and is—an unusual role for me. I didn't know if I could let go like that, but I knew that I needed to.

Georgie and I fell asleep quickly, but during the night I was suddenly aware that we were in the act of making love. I had no memory of how we got to that point, and afterward, Georgie told me that she didn't, either. Maybe I was ready to let go of what was inside.

I won't try to reconstruct that Saturday, but here are a few memories:

- I don't know what this had to do with the deaths of my uncle and aunt and the arrest of my cousin, but I asked my mother the question burning in me to be asked: Did she love my father? She answered with a story about his bad driving. I guess I got my answer.

- For the only time I can remember in my life, I sobbed unstoppably—not once, but several times.
- Some in the family room where we all sat had trouble dealing with that level of emotion. Before long, Alex said, "I've heard this before," and went to his den.
- Others let go of emotions in other ways, including the threat of a punch.
- Afterward, when we went to a local delicatessen for lunch, a chair was thrown by one of our party.
- The small personalized shiva was hard—really tense—for all of us, but I appreciated their gathering to help me through. That's what a loving family does.

Fannie had been staying in the Broomall home all week, but before Georgie and I left, she announced, "Tomorrow I have to go home."

I didn't see the logic of her returning to the empty row house on F Street. So I asked her: "Mom, why do you have to go home?"

"Because I'm afraid if I don't get on the bus Monday, I never will."

My mother had developed a routine to climb out of her years-long depression after Jack's death. She'd leave the house at nine every morning and walk to the corner, where she could take public transportation to reach Center City. Her first stop there was a thrift shop as it opened. By getting there early, she'd find the best bargains. That was her rationale. Then she'd perhaps make another stop or two as she wended her way to Thomas Jefferson University Hospital. She knew how to make friends wherever she was, so she'd become part of a group that met every day for lunch in the hospital cafeteria, where the food was reasonably priced. Then she'd return home in midafternoon.

The idea of getting on the bus—the determination to go on with life after even the worst trauma—was the gift a woman with little else to give offered to anyone who could see it in her. I used that metaphor as the theme for the eulogy I delivered at her funeral. I used it again in a sermon I gave in a Unitarian Universalist Church about New York City's recovery from 9/11.

Now it was what I had to do, too.

CHAPTER 12

SPIRITUAL INTERLUDE —NO MUD, NO LOTUS

> *Without mud you cannot have lotus flowers. Without suffering, you have no way to learn how to be understanding and compassionate.*

That's an often-cited quotation from Thich Nhat Hanh. The Sufi poet Rumi wrote:

> *The wound is the place where the Light enters you.*

The Buddhist teacher Jack Kornfield wrote:

> *Strength of the Heart comes from knowing that the pain that we each must bear is part of the greater pain shared by all that lives. It is not just "our" pain, but "the" pain and realizing this awakens our universal compassion.*

Father Richard Rohr, a Franciscan Mystic, wrote:

> *The place of the wound is the place of the greatest gift.*

and

> *Our very wounds can become sacred wounds, if we let them.*

Ram Das said:

> *Suffering is part of our training program for becoming wise.*

Pema Chödrön wrote:

> *That which can cause our destruction becomes a blessing in disguise when we let the energies arise and pass through us over and over again, without acting out.*

In the poem "Lead," by Mary Oliver, a survivor of childhood sexual abuse, she expresses with grace that pain can "break open" a heart and lead it to "never close again to the rest of the world."

CHAPTER 13

THE MOTHER OF ALL MIDLIFE CRISES

In the wake of Eddie and Margaret's death, I had a conversation with my New York cousin Ruth, Bobby's mother, in which she mentioned the possibility of a Bobby–Barry connection. She meant the possibility of some inherited trait in each of them. That was unlikely, because even though we were all in one interconnected family, the distance between the two on the family tree was large, and Bobby's father, Syd, had a brother with schizophrenia, or something like it.

But Bobby and Barry *were* connected for me, and now I was the last man standing—the last of the three of us who could live freely outside an institution with locks on the doors. I had been born with the drive not to be an imposition on the world; now I aspired to be a benefit, even if that meant sacrificing the creature comforts of my sybaritic Manhattan lifestyle. I wanted to make better use of my life.

That meant matriculating as an adult student in the New School (then called the New School for Social Research), to take night classes and explore the possibility of becoming a clinical psychologist. It might mean giving up my well-paying job at Mobil. It might mean moving from Manhattan to one of the boroughs. Georgie, who had been a loyal support through my crisis, rebelled at that.

She was in a different life stage—looking forward to retirement, unwilling to change her direction. The age difference and my life crisis had caught up to us. We soon ended our twelve-year union on friendly terms. She slept with me (without sex) on my first night in my new apartment in the Jackson Heights neighborhood of Queens.

Marathon group experiences like Werner Erhard's est (the Erhard Seminars Training) had been sweeping the culture since the early 1970s. For a time, everyone from stockbrokers to poets to suburban couples wanted to "get it"—the mysterious breakthrough promised after sixty hours of self-confrontation in a hotel ballroom. Participants sat in uncomfortable chairs for hours without breaks while a leader barked questions designed to collapse their defenses.

In my Powelton Village phase ten years earlier, my then-wife, Susie, was working on a master's degree in group dynamics, and our marriage ended on her return from a weekend-long encounter group. The marathon-weekend movement merged encounter group toughness with a superficial adaptation of gestalt therapy. Est was followed by Lifespring, Landmark Forum, and Justin Sterling's programs called Men, Sex & Power and Women, Sex & Power. Newly divorced and uncertain how to reenter the dating world, I spent a weekend with more than a hundred other guys in a high school gymnasium, mostly clothed but sometimes not, with Sterling supposedly "clarifying differences between men and women and transforming the quality of people's relationships."

What I learned was that I was *way* outside the norm in how I felt, as a man, about women, sex, and power. I hadn't understood how far I was outside the norm until, during that weekend, Sterling asked volunteers to stand before the group and describe their greatest sexual experience. I had one I wanted to share, but his failure to select me prevented what would have been a mega-embarrassment.

I would have shared the wonder of having awakened from sleep in a sex act neither I nor Georgie remembered beginning. The other guys all talked about how many orifices they had penetrated and how they had tied a woman up and returned hours later. If that means I'm a variant from the typical man, that's OK with me.

Sterling's staff sorted us by geographical residence into groups intended to meet weekly to share experiences and take on projects. Men needed to be warriors, they insisted, and in modern life that meant taking on causes and service projects. My group clicked, and these guys—Larry, Craig, and Rob are the ones I remember—became my close buddies in my new Queens existence. With Bobby and Barry in mind, I persuaded these guys to adopt as our mission the Creedmoor Psychiatric Center in Queens Village. With some fifty drab buildings—many now vacant and covered with bird droppings—spread over three hundred acres, Creedmoor was, and is, a nightmare.

I imagined Bobby living in a nightmare like this as my Men, Sex & Power friends and I cleaned filthy marble lobbies in which urine and excrement had been thrown, gave parties with Cokes and cookies for barely functional patients, and paid holiday visits to a group home. We were ministering to the least of these, a group that included my two childhood age-mates, to whom I could not minister in person. For both, I would be a painful reminder of the life they couldn't live. For one of them, it was a reminder of the two lives he had taken.

As I write this section, I'm awakening to the role that the Creedmore service played in beginning my emotional and spiritual ascent from my lifetime low point. I wish I could hug each member of the Queens Men, Sex & Power group for joining me in getting a start toward devoting my life to others.

In 1986, one of the group members, who serviced computers, offered me a deal on a new IBM XT computer. Although home computers were still rare, I thought it would be fun to buy one for word processing and to learn more about using it. After he delivered it and left, I took it out of the box, struggled to figure out how to attach the keyboard and monitor to the processor, and plugged it in. In a few minutes, I was looking at a blank greenish screen with only a single right-pointing white caret blinking in the upper left corner.

I hadn't realized that I'd need software, a printer, an external disk drive, and books of instruction. I visited a computer store, bought bagsful of stuff, returned to my Jackson Heights apartment, and taught myself, first, how to use DOS.

DOS stands for Disk Operating System, a family of command-line operating systems that managed files, programs, and hardware on early IBM PC–compatible machines. That blinking white caret indicated the command line. I needed to learn which commands to type in order to get the computer to do anything.

If I had written off what I paid for the computer and waited until operating systems with a GUI (graphical user interface) were more common, I would have saved both money and headaches . . . and perhaps avoided the midlife crisis from Hell. It wasn't the IBM XT's fault, but let's pretend it was.

Understanding the link from the computer to the crisis involves another group member, Craig. His day job was as a physician's assistant in a methadone clinic in Manhattan, but he also trained both emergency responders and scuba divers.

I accepted his invitation to learn scuba and became an ardent advanced diver until a form of asthma required me to stop in the 1990s. Three years earlier, I had met a fellow diver named Stan who recruited me as his assistant running a scuba forum on an internet messaging platform called GEnie.

Early forums like CompuServe and GEnie were nothing like today's social media. The dial-up modem in this photo is more modern than what we used then, and we used our keyboards to type in commands and messages.

The systems operator (sysop) of a forum received payment for the minutes users spent in that forum. The assistant sysop (me, in this scuba forum) got to use the platform for free. Being the sysop of a busy forum could be a full-time job, and the Atari forum on GEnie was busy, so its sysop, whom I'll call Julie, was online a lot. We were making our forums lively and encouraging users to read and post.

I apologize for the complicated background, but an online romance developed between Julie and me, well before online romances became a thing. To communicate with someone on another GEnie forum required typing in a "notify" command. If I remember the format, it was something like:

> *n/ julie: What do you do when you're not working at the computer?*

She could reply with:

> *n/ melhpine: I hang out on the beach and paint.*

Julie could be elusive and hard to pin down, which added to the intrigue. Eventually, she explained that she ran a successful mobile plumbing company in addition to the Atari forum and sometimes set up an easel on the beach near her home and painted. She said she was single with no children but often cared for her sister's.

Eventually, a villain, who happened to be named Barry, entered the picture, and she escaped his grasp long enough to fly to New York and live with me for two weeks before vanishing. I'll spare myself the embarrassment of explaining more.

The picture she had sent me and her position on GEnie were both real. Everything else was a fantasy she had constructed to divert herself from a life that was intolerable, but even as the truth emerged, I wouldn't let her go, and we discussed actually getting together.

Here's where her real life stood at the end of June 1988:

Julie and her husband, Bob, had four children, ages four to eight. Living with them was Julie's daughter Lucy, sixteen. When Lucy was twelve, Bob was arrested for molesting her, but Julie told the police that Lucy had made up the story, so Bob was released. When Julie told Lucy about me, something about that led Lucy to admit that Bob was currently molesting her. She had retracted the previous story out of fear that she'd be put into foster care.

Julie called the local police to make an appointment for Lucy to give a statement on Friday, June 1. She told Bob that he couldn't come home. When she then called me, the urge to be a rescuer took over. I didn't trust Julie to handle the situation and thought that maybe I could add a bit of support for Lucy to make the statement. I asked Julie if her daughter would be comfortable with my accompanying them to the police station. Lucy and I had never met, but when Julie asked her, Lucy said yes.

I dropped everything and flew cross-country to be with them. As I drove them home after Lucy's meeting with the police officer and approached their house, a pickup truck passed us going in the other direction. I noticed that the driver looked grim and dazed. Julie said it was Bob, who had a weird, determined look on his face. Lucy was in the back seat, and Julie didn't explain, but I got the hint.

Bob had left a note—clearly a suicide note. It's hard to get police to take a suicide note seriously, and we learned it was especially hard on the July Fourth weekend. I remained with the family for the weekend. On Sunday, July 3, the deputy coroner arrived to tell Julie that Bob's body had been found in the cab of his truck with a hose leading up from the exhaust pipe.

I know it's hard to believe, but I married Julie five weeks later, on August 8, 1988. I bought a house for us on the East Coast, and moved her and her children into it in the fall. I understand now how that gave me the illusion of filling the void I felt inside.

Late the next year, I discovered I had far more debts than I could pay. Julie had forged my name to open charge accounts and run up debts, then hidden the bills. I filed for divorce and learned that the laws in the state where we lived made almost no exceptions to holding one spouse responsible for the debts of the other. Eventually, I filed for bankruptcy.

It wasn't the fault of that IBM XT. My urge to rescue a family drove my temporary insanity.

And that required me to redefine myself. I was no longer someone who doesn't get scammed, and I was no longer someone who always paid his bills. I was still childless, though. Even though I had joint custody of the four young children, Julie had disappeared with them—into Canada.

CHAPTER 14

SPIRITUAL INTERLUDE —SELF-COMPASSION, GENEROSITY, AND SPIRITUALITY

"The Protective Role of Self-Compassion in Trauma Recovery and Its Moderating Impact on Post-Traumatic Symptoms and Post-Traumatic Growth" is the title of a March 9, 2025, article in *Nature* magazine. The title tells the whole story. When trauma survivors practice self-compassion, they can experience significant post-traumatic growth even while dealing with intense symptoms.

In a study of 413 adults who had been through trauma, the story reported, those with more self-compassion grew from the experience. They found new meaning, developed deeper relationships, and discovered inner strengths. In other words, severe trauma may enhance your psychological and spiritual well-being *if* you have compassion for yourself as you rebound.

The idea of self-compassion shows up repeatedly in published studies as playing a positive role in recovery after traumas. Another study, published February 11, 2020, in the *European Journal of Psychotraumatology*, found similar results for 492 students four and a half years after earthquakes in China's Sichuan Province.

Social scientists have given the name post-traumatic growth to the positive changes they have observed in people who have struggled with the aftermath of traumas:

- Greater appreciation for life
- Closer relationships
- Increased personal strength
- Recognition of new possibilities
- Spiritual development

In that fifth category, trauma survivors tend to deepen their faith, strengthen their spiritual practice, or reach a philosophical understanding of life's meaning.

Serving others is a form of recognizing new possibilities and developing spiritually. Dr. Cortland Dahl and Dr. Richard Davidson, of the Center for Healthy Minds at the University of Wisconsin–Madison, have written:

> *From a neuroscience perspective, generosity and compassion activate the brain's reward circuitry. When people behave generously in laboratory studies, the neural reward network lights up more strongly than when they receive something for themselves.*

They also cite studies from Johns Hopkins University that followed older adults participating in Experience Corps Baltimore between 1999 and the late 2000s, where volunteers fifty-five and older served at least fifteen hours a week helping children in urban elementary schools. The volunteers' physical health improved, as did their memory and cognitive executive functions.

A Google or AI search will provide plenty of anecdotal examples of a spiritual practice aiding recovery from trauma, often in first-person articles and books like this one. Any scientific study on the subject, however, is close to impossible because of the wide variations in spiritual practices and their intensity.

Incarceration is a trauma, and researchers can evaluate the prison population more closely than they can the free population. The literature consistently shows that spiritual engagement during incarceration can be a meaningful component of rehabilitation, particularly when inmates actively participate rather than simply attend programs passively.

Studies have found that faith-based programming contributes to identity transformation, an increased sense of meaning and purpose in life, "virtue development," reduced negative emotions, and a decreased risk of interpersonal aggression. One Brazilian study comparing faith-based and vocational training prisons found the faith-based facility had a 16 percent recidivism rate compared with 36 percent for the vocational training over three years.

Studies like these can't be definitive guides for all of us, but together with the anecdotal evidence (not to mention logic), they show that self-compassion, generosity toward others, and a spiritual practice work together to heal those who are suffering.

CHAPTER 15

BORN THIRTY-FIVE

As a young adult, I'd sometimes say that I was born thirty-five years old. From a Buddhist perspective, though, I was born with equanimity. Teachers thought I was exceptionally well behaved when I didn't jump and reach for the best trinket being handed out. I wasn't especially well behaved; I just had no interest in shiny trinkets.

Another way to see that might be childhood depression, but it existed in me from birth. I now think it was the karma—or the epigenetic heritage—of having been born from a womb that didn't want me, into a heritage of starvation and oppression. I was a baby who wanted to eat—a lot. The response to my crying so much was to feed me. Once I was able to feed myself, I didn't want much else. According to my mother, when I was four or five, she asked me why I didn't hit back when a playmate hit me as we played outside, and I replied, "If I hit him, then he'll hit me, and I'll hit him, and he'll hit me."

Was I born with the wisdom of an oppressed heritage?

In the late 1940s and early '50s, immigrant parents didn't "protect" their children from harsh realities. At least mine didn't. Although an uncle erupted in rage at the mention of anything German, I remember no emotion when the subject of the Holocaust came up with my parents. But they didn't avoid it. I knew that my father had left his closest brother, Leibel, and his sister Chaske behind. I didn't know yet exactly what had happened to them nor how to ask. That was one of the many answers I'd never hear directly from him.

Jack and Fannie joined the local synagogue, Congregation Brith Israel, at D Street and Roosevelt Boulevard, as I turned six so they could enroll me in Hebrew school there. Jewish boys got their religious schooling on Sunday morning and after school twice a week. We learned Jewish religious practices and Hebrew, leading to our bar mitzvahs at age thirteen. Many girls attended, too, but bat mitzvahs for them were not yet common.

The building that housed Brith Israel was built around 1930. It's now home to the New Life Church–Philly, a diverse Christian church that describes itself as a "thriving family in the city where the broken from all nations are made alive and whole, finding hope and purpose in Christ." In a neighborhood that was close to 100 percent white when I lived there—with immigrants from Eastern Europe, Ireland, and Italy—it aims to reflect the current demographics: 57 percent African American, 22 percent Hispanic, 15 percent Asian, 4 percent white.

In other words, the neighborhood hasn't changed—filled with individuals and families working hard for a better future, to be let in to the American Dream. As houses of worship in such urban neighborhoods pass from one faith to another, the

new occupants can seldom afford much renovation. So the focus of the New Life–Philly sanctuary is what once was a *bimah*—Hebrew for the stage or raised platform with the Ark containing the Torah at the center. Hebrew lettering is still visible.

I was bar mitzvahed on that *bimah* on May 2, 1959, the same day as a far more significant event in Tallahassee, Florida. Three white men and a white sixteen-year-old boy kidnapped and raped Betty Jean Owens, a nineteen-year-old African American woman. What made that event especially significant for the South was that an all-white jury convicted the four and sentenced them to life in prison.

On Brith Israel's *bimah* that day, I chanted the blessings and the Haftara reading I had been assigned. While the Torah is a scroll containing the first five books of the Old Testament, the Haftara is another scroll containing selections from Prophets. The Shamus (a synagogue official) chanted that day's designated portion of the Torah, and the bar mitzvah boy—me—chanted the designated portion of the Haftara. This was what I had been trained for over six years.

After concluding my portion of the service, I got to sit on one of the high-backed upholstered armchairs on the bimah—the one alongside the president of the congregation, whose name was Mr. Ulster. I vividly remember the big book of

Haftara readings Mr. Ulster had in his lap as I took my seat on his right. He leaned over to me and spoke into my left ear: "Is dis what you was reading?"

He pointed to a section in the book on his lap. I was too flustered to read what he pointed to, and I wasn't used to reading Hebrew without the vows, as it was printed in books for grown-ups, so I just said yes, after which he continued into my left ear: "Dat was terrible!"

That (or dat) was not why I left Judaism. I remember being uncomfortable with the term "chosen people" the first time I heard it. I didn't want to be part of a group from which others were excluded. And I found ridiculous the idea that girls and women didn't count the same as boys and men in God's holy abacus. I had not yet read George Orwell's *Animal Farm,* which was published in the United States in the year of my birth, but I had a visceral revulsion at any suggestion that *All animals are equal, but some animals are more equal than others.*

Nevertheless, I might have continued to identify Judaism as my religion and eventually find a comfortable home in a Reform, Reconstructionist, Humanistic, or Renewal congregation were it not for a rabbi whose name I have forgotten. He led Brith Israel when I was sixteen.

For the sake of my mother, I fulfilled many of the obligations traditional for at least one immediate family member of a deceased person. A particularly important ceremony was Yizkor on Yom Kippur, the most solemn day in the Jewish calendar. The Yizkor service was for congregants who had lost at least one parent. But there was a problem, one common for High Holiday services during the 1950s. Attending Rosh Hashanah and Yom Kippur services required a ticket, which required a membership in the congregation, which we couldn't afford.

Since Jack's death, Fannie and I had lived on the Social Security payments for an unremarried widow with a child, what she could make babysitting, and what I could make after school as a messenger for a watch repairer. We could not afford to be members of the congregation. Because of Yizkor's importance, the rabbi offered it once during Yom Kippur in a special service for nonmembers. As I sat in the first row for that service, my cheeks burned with embarrassment as the rabbi castigated the attendees for not being members. Although I don't remember his name, I'll never forget one sentence:

Rabbis have to eat, too, you know.

After Barry killed Eddie and Margaret, I decided to find a religion where I might fit. Every civilization had had a religion, I thought, so I'd find one for me. I didn't believe in a God as portrayed in the Abrahamic faiths, and despite what that Holiness minister had told me when I was twenty, I still had no idea how someone of European descent living in the West could practice the religion I suspected made sense.

I attended services at a few churches that never felt right. I had a friend I'll call Diane who was deeply religious and married to an Episcopal priest I'll call Phil.

I felt a bond with Diane, in part because of a horror we had gone through together in 1977. She was a researcher for the senior writers at Mobil Corporation, with an office a few doors along a hallway from mine. Our windows faced north on Forty-Second Street between Third and Lexington Avenues. We would often pop into each other's offices. Around 10 a.m. on Wednesday, August 3, she came in saying, "Did you hear that boom outside?"

I replied, "Yeah, it was just a truck backfire. I hear them all the time and think they're gunshots."

"No! Look out your window!"

She was right. Workers in the Chrysler Building across Forty-Second Street had opened windows and were looking down toward our lobby, six floors below us. Traffic was slowing down, and smoke was visible. I don't remember which of us said, *Let's go see what happened!*

Like a couple of idiots, we took an elevator to the lobby, which was filled with smoke, and walked through it onto the sidewalk. Or at least I did. I don't remember when Diana and I parted. When, again in idiocy, I turned to reenter the lobby, a security guard waved me back outside. Having left the building, I never heard the announcement to evacuate, with instructions to walk down the stairs to the back doors on Forty-First Street.

That left me alone on Forty-Second Street with a few Human Relations Department employees who had been in the office where the bomb went off. I knew one of the women, whom I'll call Linda. She was hysterical, and nothing I could do calmed her. Here's what had happened:

That office, with a plate-glass window facing the street, handled the hiring of temporary employees. Anyone could enter through the lobby and apply. Charles Steinberg—who was twenty-six and lived in the same apartment building as I did, nine blocks away—had an appointment with Linda to offer the services of the temporary employment agency he co-owned.

As he was meeting with Linda, a woman entered the reception area through the lobby, took an employment application, put her handbag on the coat rack, and sat down. After appearing to work on her application, she left, saying she had changed her mind. The receptionist said she couldn't take Mobil's employment application with her and retrieved it. Minutes later, the bomb in her handbag exploded. A fingerprint on the application identified her as twenty-two-year-old Marie Haydee Beltran Torres, a Puerto Rican nationalist who would later be convicted and sentenced to life in prison.

The blast killed my neighbor Steinberg and wounded seven others as he sat at Linda's desk. No wonder I couldn't calm her.

If I had looked through the shattered window, I would have seen his body, but I was focused on the survivors.

Four miles to the south, Georgie was working in the newsroom of the *New York Post* with the constant sound of police radios coming from within feet of her desk. She heard the emergency calls that ambulances and more ambulances were needed at the Mobil Building and the request for the bomb squad and its disposal unit. With telephone service to midtown disrupted and no service at all to the Mobil Building, we had no way to contact each other.

When I was ready to leave the scene of the crime, I walked one block east to the Daily News Building, where I had worked until fourteen months earlier, took the elevator to the seventh floor, and strode into the newsroom. I had no useful information for my former colleagues, but they didn't object when I took a seat and started trying to get a call through to Georgie.

As we approached our apartment building after meeting on a street corner and deciding to go straight home, we recognized the scrum of reporters and photographers outside the entrance to the lobby. What the hell was going on? What sort of trouble had followed us home? By asking the reporters, we learned that the bombing had killed Steinberg and just then saw his widow half-escorted, half-carried into the building.

In addition to the look on her face, what I remember most about the aftermath is how, even though I first identified the sound of the blast as a harmless truck backfire, for months to come I would leap involuntarily at any sudden, sharp sound, like that of a door closing.

The bombing of the Mobil Building wasn't a major trauma, a turning point, among the others in my life, but they all have had a cumulative effect, each leaving its mark. As I wrote about it, some of the memories and emotions from almost fifty years ago returned as though they happened last month. I did some research into what, to me, was the most remarkable effect—how any sharp sound evoked an exaggerated startle response in me for months afterward, even though I didn't identify the sound of the bomb as a danger when it happened.

It's a heightened state of response called "hyperarousal" or "hypervigilance." We're used to hearing about it in stories of war veterans suffering post-traumatic stress disorder (PTSD), but it deserves more attention in less-extraordinary traumas. A 1987 Bureau of Justice Statistics report remains the standard for estimating the lifetime likelihood of being a violent crime victim. At the then-current crime rate, five out of every six Americans are likely to experience violent crime in their lifetimes.

The brain's threat-detection system (particularly the amygdala) becomes hypersensitive after trauma. Your nervous system wants to protect you but can't distinguish between actual threats and harmless loud sounds. The way our bodies "remember" trauma persists in a physical and involuntary way. You're jumping or ducking before you realize that the sound, sight, or other stimulus was harmless.

Various sorts of therapy and medication can help. I've had countless years of therapy and expect to continue taking antidepressants for the rest of my life. But it's my spiritual arc that has brought me to equanimity, joy, compassion, and clarity. There's no separation between what we call sacred and what we call profane.

The Dutch Catholic priest Henri Nouwen wrote:

> *The spiritual life does not remove us from the world but leads us deeper into it.*

I thought of Diane and her husband as people to visit as I searched for a church home in the mid-1980s. Phil was pastor of a church an hour's drive from my home, which was then in Queens. Might I fit in as an Episcopalian? I decided to give his church a try and called, asking if I could spend a weekend with them. They said yes. Soon after the start of the next Sunday morning service, we stood and read what I, raised Jewish, had never heard before. It begins:

> *We believe in one God,*
> *the Father, the Almighty,*
> *maker of heaven and earth,*
> *of all that is, seen and unseen.*
>
> *We believe in one Lord, Jesus Christ,*
> *the only Son of God,*
> *eternally begotten of the Father,*
> *God from God, Light from Light,*
> *true God from true God,*
> *begotten, not made,*
> *of one Being with the Father.*

I wanted so much to have a religion, and liked Phil so much, that I tried to find ways I could accept those words as true. As we ate brunch in his parsonage after the service, I asked him, "You know those words you say at the beginning—'We believe this, We believe that'? I can define those words for myself, can't I?"

He replied, "That's called a creed. We say the Nicene Creed at the beginning of every Sunday morning service. If you can't define the words the way we define them, then you're not an Episcopalian."

Was it naive of me to be shocked, hearing those words from someone I respected? The message I heard was:

> *All animals are equal, but some animals are more equal than others.*

He could preach that we're all equal under God and could socialize with me as an equal, but I can't sit as a member of his congregation unless I define words the way his religion says they should be defined? I expressed none of that before leaving after brunch, hurt and yet accepting that I was not an Episcopalian.

Then I remembered that, during the Vietnam era, Unitarian Universalist churches were friendly, so I looked into them. Because it was in a convenient location, I called the Community Church of New York to request pamphlets. When they arrived, the one on top of the bundle said: "A Church Without a Creed." Then, when I attended my first Sunday service, the Reverend Bruce Southworth hooked me further, devoting the service to Vesak, the celebration of the Buddha's birth. The hook sunk deeper when I noticed the inscription on the building:

> *Deeds, not Creeds*

I think it was at that service that Bruce announced the coming talk by the Vietnamese Buddhist monk and author Thich Nhat Hanh. I bought Nhat Hanh's book *The Miracle of Mindfulness,* attended more of his talks, read more, and began learning how to be a Buddhist in the West.

That gave me a boost toward climbing out of the chasm I had fallen into after Barry's confession, but additional boulders would fall before my spiritual awakening.

CHAPTER 16

SPIRITUAL INTERLUDE —OUR ISLAND OF REFUGE

Living life is a spiritual act.

Sometimes, we're aware of the sacredness of the tree outside our widow even when the branches are bare. Sometimes, we recognize the miracle of taking another breath or another step. Some of us are aware more often than others. Some are never aware.

In *Conjectures of a Guilty Bystander*, Thomas Merton wrote:

> *Here is an unspeakable secret: Paradise is all around us and we do not understand.*

As you'll read in later chapters, I came to believe—to be certain, in fact—that I live in a pure land, a place where, to quote a song by Peter Mayer, everything is holy now. The route from sitting on the floor listening to "Hey Jude" to there was by no means smooth, but I'm grateful for every moment of it.

There are roughly as many fake Buddha quotes as there are fake Lincoln and Einstein quotes put together. Some are variations on the theme of living in the present moment. There's no credible translation of the Buddha saying that in a pithy aphorism suitable for a social media meme, but here's what he *did* say in verse—twice—in the Bhaddekaratta Sutta:

You shouldn't chase after the past
or place expectations on the future.
What is past
is left behind.
The future
is as yet unreached.
Whatever quality is present
you clearly see right there,
right there.
Not taken in,
unshaken,
that's how you develop the heart.
Ardently doing
what should be done today,
for—who knows?— tomorrow
death.
There is no bargaining
with Mortality & his mighty horde.

Whoever lives thus ardently,
relentlessly
both day & night,
has truly had an auspicious day:
so says the Peaceful Sage.

The Roman emperor and Stoic philosopher Marcus Aurelius said:

> *Give yourself a gift: the present moment.*

And here's the noted psychologist Abraham Maslow:

> *The ability to be in the present moment is a major component of mental wellness.*

Part of my spiritual practice is reciting this verse from Thich Nhat Hanh on awakening every morning:

> *Waking up this morning I smile,*
> *Twenty-four brand new hours before me.*
> *I vow to live fully in each moment,*
> *And to see beings through eyes of compassion.*

The present moment is a safe place. It's entirely your own to make of it what you will. It's a refuge from whatever storms surround you. I never understood that until I lived with a steady stream of debt collectors calling and the sheriff knocking on my door to serve a summons. After my bankruptcy lawyer advised me to stop paying all bills, the deluge began. I was ashamed, embarrassed, and feeling a need to adjust to a new definition of who I was. I cringed when the phone rang.

Then I realized that nothing stopped me from enjoying *Cheers* and *Murphy Brown* on television. That slice of pizza tasted just the same as it had before. The present moment doesn't need to reflect embarrassment about the past or worries about the future.

It is a safe haven.

CHAPTER 17

TWO MORE DEATHS AND A NEW OUTLOOK

I was fortunate to be an adult with a television during the 1978–83 run of the TV series *Taxi*, with an outstanding ensemble, including Judd Hirsch, Danny DeVito, Marilu Henner, Tony Danza, Andy Kaufman, Christopher Lloyd, Carol Kane, and Rhea Perlman. If you've never watched it, start from the beginning if you can find it. The cabdrivers, their supervisor (DeVito), and some of their love interests will bring you to laughter, occasional tears, and insights into human nature.

With my Powelton Village background, I always wanted more screen time for the character Jim Ignatowski, played brilliantly by Lloyd. His version of a burned-out hippie was gloriously weird in a way that somehow made perfect sense—*to him*. His backstory: He was once a brilliant Harvard student named James Caldwell who took one too many drugs in the '60s and emerged on the other side as "Ignatowski"—a name supposedly revealed to him in the mirror as "Star Taxi" spelled backward.

Lloyd played him with beautiful sincerity. Jim was more than a punchline. Breaking through his fried brain cells and spacey demeanor, he had moments of genuine wisdom and sweetness. He might say something profound and follow it up with something incomprehensible.

My cousin Jay could have been the prototype for Jim. Jay and I renewed our friendship a decade after our Temple University days. The Jay who had left Philadelphia with his first wife to make and sell jewelry around the country had returned and would visit me in my apartment on his weekly business trips to Manhattan. I soon began to return the visits. Here's a Jim-like anecdote he told me about himself: "I went to Macy's to buy a new shirt and couldn't find a salesperson to help me. So I stood in the aisle and shouted, 'Help' I kept shouting, 'Help!' 'Help!' 'Help!' louder and louder until a salesperson arrived."

As I remember that, I can't help thinking, "WWJD?" What would Jim do (have done)? Probably something similar. As with Jay, it would have been done in calm friendliness, an attitude of: Isn't this how life is supposed to work?

Jay followed a macrobiotic diet and the *sanpaku* face-reading teachings of George Ohsawa—that a person's health could be determined by the proportion of white in the eyes above and below the iris. Jay followed a macrobiotic diet if you ignore the frozen Sara Lee chocolate cake he was addicted to or the cigarettes he smoked. It's not the cigarettes that kill you, he said, but the cigarettes in combination with bad eating habits. He died at age fifty.

In his new life, Jay was married to a woman named Janet, a ceramic artist. This vegetarian couple had bought an abandoned butcher shop on South Second Street in Philly and converted it into a comfortable residence, with the meat locker as the master bedroom.

Jay had become obsessed with making money in the women's clothing business. On his weekly trips to New York City, he'd buy odd lots in the Seventh Avenue clothing district—the eight blouses here and twelve dresses there left over after manufacturers had filled much larger orders from retail chains. He'd load them into his van and sell them for cash—always cash—to small shops in the Philly area. On his New York trips, he entered into a partnership with a Chinatown entrepreneur who employed women in basement factories to duplicate fashion items Jay supplied.

I was sure that my beloved, inspired cousin would never be involved in running a sweatshop, but I never asked about the working conditions. I probably should have. One of the practices that has helped me to wisdom is called Chöd, Tibetan for "cutting" or "cutting through." It often refers to cutting our attachment to our egos, but it can also involve growing spiritually by doing the things we consider most difficult. After studying Chöd, I'm more willing to ask the questions I would once have found difficult, like "Jay, what are the conditions like for the women who work in your partner's sewing factory?"

In my midlife crisis, as I became obsessed with Julie, I lost touch with Jay.

The divorce and bankruptcy happened as my job moved from New York to Northern Virginia. The loss of contact with the four young children and my mother's death came soon after. I had no need for a "Check Your Stress Level" questionnaire. I knew the answer. But I had learned to find safety in the present moment.

The good news was that Mobil's relocation allowance was generous. It didn't take much cash or credit for me to move into a rented apartment in Leesburg, Virginia, in June 1990. And the Unitarian Universalist Church in Reston became my outside-of-work community. I quickly made supportive relationships there, but once Julie disappeared with the four young children, I made suicide plans. I even bought the revolver and ammunition.

I had legal and financial details to tie up and a singalong to run at the UU church in May 1991, so I set the date for my death as a week or so after the singalong. Without admitting my suicide plan on my application for the program, I became a responder on the Northern Virginia Hotline, with an office in a secret location in Arlington. My reasoning was that I could empathize with people in crisis, and I succeeded in talking down at least one man who said he was standing on a chair with a noose around his neck.

In September, I met Carol Harkrader and her four-year-old son, Thomas, at the Reston church's new-member orientation. Having firm suicide plans put me in a gray zone—wanting the warmth of relationships but cautious about generating enough warmth myself to entice others to become attached to me. I knew immediately that, under other circumstances, I'd want to date her. But that seemed irresponsible and selfish.

On Sunday, October 21, I had to skip the second session of the Reston new-member orientation so that I could spend the day with my hospitalized mother before her open-heart surgery. I stayed with her that evening and arrived back before five thirty the next morning. As hospital personnel wheeled her from her room—always one to crack a joke, even one borrowed from George Burns—she said, "I guess today I better not buy any green bananas."

In my own dark-humor style, I replied, "Mom, if I were you, today I wouldn't buy any yellow bananas."

Those were the last words we said to each other. Marilyn, Alex, Ginger, and I sat in the waiting room as the surgeon twice told us of failed attempts to start her heart pumping again on its own. Finally, we all agreed that we'd let her die. I was the only one of us who asked to enter the operating room to see her body. I kissed her, on the cheek, and was surprised that it felt good. I have no memory before that of either of us ever having kissed the other.

Carol and Thomas lived in Leesburg, so after returning from my mother's funeral and shiva, I'd sometimes offer the two a ride to church. Then the unexpected happened. Carol asked me out. She had tickets to a dance matinee at the Kennedy Center in Washington, DC. Still getting used to taking speed limits seriously after twenty years of New York living, I got a speeding ticket on my way to the city. On the way back, I offered to take her to dinner, so we picked up Thomas and went to a Chinese restaurant in Leesburg.

Although I went through the motions that evening of being on a date, I actually felt as though I was wrapped in an impermeable emotional membrane. Certain that I would soon be dead, I didn't want to feel anything and wanted to prevent anyone else from feeling anything toward me.

But then another unexpected thing happened. In April, Jay's older brother called to tell me that Jay had died of heart disease.

After I drove to the Philadelphia area for his memorial service, I learned that he had begun to withdraw from the world into depression and agoraphobia, the fear of going out into the world. He had abandoned his business and failed to pay his debts. Although he knew he had a serious heart disease, he remained in bed constantly and refused to follow the advice of Western medicine.

Years back, his first wife told me: "When Jay goes out to buy a pack of cigarettes, you won't see him again for hours. He gets into long conversations with everyone he meets."

Now he had died after isolating himself.

Days later, I left the converted butcher shop that Janet and her children now shared without Jay, to return to Northern Virginia. I had cut myself off from emotional contact with others because of my suicide plan. It seemed selfish of me to deepen any relationship, but I needed something warm to return to. I wanted something to look forward to during the three-and-a-half-hour drive to Leesburg.

I remembered that the Chinese restaurant where Carol, Thomas, and I had enjoyed dinner together held an oldies music night on Fridays. Carol had asked me out that time. Now it was my turn, and I didn't want to wait for an answer. As soon as I was out of the city, I pulled over at a phone booth and called Carol.

"Hi, Carol. It's Mel, calling from a phone booth. I've been in Philadelphia because my cousin Jay died. I'm returning from his memorial service and want something to look forward to when I get back. You know that Chinese restaurant in Leesburg where we had dinner? They have an oldies night on Fridays. Would you like to go this week?"

"That sounds like fun. I've seen those advertisements. Let's try it. How old was your cousin?"

"It's very sad. He had a wife and two young children. He was just fifty."

"What did he die of?"

"He had a heart condition but believed in macrobiotics and wouldn't accept Western medicine. He also got depressed, stopped working, and withdrew into his bedroom."

"You said he had a wife and two small children? And he stopped working and refused a doctor's care?"

"Yes. It's so sad."

"If he was my husband, he wouldn't have died of heart disease. . . . I would have killed him first."

That wasn't the dose of warmth I expected, but I appreciated the directness and the humor. Looking back, I also appreciate the message to wake up and stop seeing Jay—or myself—as a victim. I had received a message like that once before, when I had consulted a lawyer about what Julie had done to me.

After the lawyer read a letter I had sent him, he looked at me across his desk and said, "If half the things you've said in the letter are true, you've been treated horribly. But I see you sitting there being a victim. If you're ever to get over it, you have to stop being a victim."

It took more spiritual maturity before I fully understood the futility of victimhood, but I was beginning to. Carol's crack was another push in that direction. Here's a crude way of expressing a spiritual truth that won't make its way into any collection of inspirational quotations:

Life is shit and then you die, but we all have agency over how we shovel the shit.

Carol and I continued to date after that Friday night, and we broke through the impermeable membrane around my emotions. It started that night. She'd say afterward that she was impressed that I began dancing with her before the drinks arrived. She had a membrane of her own to remove, the residue of a husband who had deceived her about money. We had that in common.

The singalong that May at the Reston church was based on the music from the show *South Pacific*, and I had recruited Carol to lead the congregation's children in "Dites-Moi." I recruited a petite woman in her eighties to wear a grass skirt as the congregation sang "Honey Bun" to her.

I was in no hurry to use my six-shooter afterward. I straightened out some remaining credit hassles, donated the gun to the Leesburg Police Department, and moved into Carol's house.

We got married in May 1992. A year later, I adopted Thomas, and the three of us took the last name Pine and the middle name Harkrader. At the same time, and with no additional fee or hassle, I shortened my first name to Mel.

I often joked that my parents had been poor and too tired to give me a middle name. It wasn't entirely a joke. Ginger was Stanley Irwin Pine. Marilyn was Marilyn Naomi Pine. Had they run out of energy? enthusiasm? creativity? caring? love? I couldn't blame them for "Melvin," though. A Dean Martin and Jerry Lewis routine in the 1950s made it an object of laughter, so I was glad to get rid of the "vin" while I was legally changing my name anyway.

"For the same price, I changed my first name to Mel."

That's how I described it to friends. But, joking aside, something deeper was going on. I was filling a gap and signaling to my new in-laws that I respected their family.

I learned about commitment from Carol. The son of a mother who didn't want me and who didn't love her husband, I hadn't taken marriage vows to heart. Susie and I had gotten married for no reason other than we had been living together for a year. I had married Julie to justify why I had a better life than Bobby and Barry. Georgie and I had committed to each other for as long as our different life stages didn't get in the way.

Carol and I did a lot of quarreling early in our time living together. Two adults in our forties, we were used to having control over our living situations. When our battles became especially intense, I'd raise the possibility of splitting up. Finally, she expressed something that at first sounded foreign: "I want you to promise me you'll never say that again. We don't break up just because we had a fight. We're committed to working things out."

Some changes take a long time. This one didn't. As soon as I made that promise to myself and her, I understood what I never before had promised. When Carol and I married, it was with the commitment to work out whatever problems might come between us. As I write this, we're eighteen months from our thirty-fifth anniversary.

CHAPTER 18

SPIRITUAL INTERLUDE —LOVE OF FATE

Amor fati, which is Latin for "love of fate," encourages us to embrace whatever lies ahead, not just tolerate it. You could call it a radical acceptance of what has happened and what *will* happen. If an event is unpleasant or painful, we welcome what we can learn from it.

Stoicism, the Greco-Roman philosophy founded by Zeno of Citium around 300 BCE, laid the groundwork for amor fati. It emphasizes distinguishing between what we can control and what we can't (external events, or fate). Stoics, such as Epictetus and Marcus Aurelius, believed we should welcome fate because it's part of the universe's rational order. A key quotation from Epictetus:

> *Don't demand that things happen as you wish, but wish that they happen as they do, and you will go on well.*

Marcus Aurelius, the Roman emperor and Stoic philosopher, echoes the sentiment:

> *Accept the things to which fate binds you, and love the people with whom fate brings you together, but do so with all your heart.*

Friedrich Nietzsche coined and popularized the term "amor fati" in works like *The Gay Science* and *Ecce Homo.* For Nietzsche, it affirms life, especially in his thought experiment on "eternal recurrence"—the idea that one must live one's life an infinite number of times in exactly the same way. Amor fati is not resignation but a joyous "yes" to existence, including suffering.

In *The Gay Science*, where he introduces the idea of eternal recurrence, Nietzsche presents it as a hypothetical scenario:

> *What if a demon were to creep after you one day or night . . . and say to you: "This life as you now live it and have lived it, you will have to live once more and innumerable times more"?*

Nietzsche wanted us to consider whether we love our lives so completely that we'd willingly relive every moment again, exactly as it was, forever. This was his ultimate measure of whether someone had reached amor fati.

Nietzsche considered Christianity nihilistic for devaluing human life in favor of a "true world" beyond it, and he admired what he saw as Buddhism's psychological sophistication. He viewed the Buddha as a kind of physician of the soul who had developed practical methods for dealing with suffering through mental discipline and detachment. But he ultimately also found Buddhism nihilistic because it seeks to eliminate suffering by eliminating both desire and attachment. Nietzsche wanted to affirm life completely, including its suffering.

I prefer to work on eliminating suffering—at least the kind we let our minds create.

CHAPTER 19

BECOMING GOOD AT THIS?

> *The call comes in the night, a hand fumbles for the light.*

That line is from a song called "Bridges" by my good friend the singer-songwriter Andrew McKnight. He wrote it in collaboration with the musician Jon Carroll as Andrew considered the impending birth of his first child. In his wisdom and compassion, he identified with parents of the past, present, and future who hear the phone as they sleep, with no way of knowing whether the call will bring joy or tears.

If you've read this far, you'll know why the line resonated the moment I heard it. I knew what it was like for a midnight call from my brother to bring tears. My midmorning call to Alice's husband Brian's office was another source of tears. I would not volunteer to go through that kind of trauma, but each instance left me stronger, more compassionate, and wiser about life's surprises. That strength, compassion, and wisdom helped me—and maybe those around me—through two more sudden tragedies.

The next one was a phone call in the early evening of Monday, September 27, 2010. It was my niece Linda telling me that her parents, my sister, Marilyn, and her husband, Alex, had been in an automobile accident. It was serious, she said, and her critically injured father was in a trauma center. Then she added, "Mom didn't make it to the hospital."

I repeated it back to her: "Mom didn't make it to the hospital?"

In a firm and steady voice, understanding the shock I must have felt, she confirmed: "Mom didn't make it to the hospital."

Marilyn was dead, and Alex had little chance of survival.

Our mother, Fannie, had died in October 1990 during open-heart surgery. It was not a surprise. In fact, I think she expected it, an impression confirmed in the discussion she and I had in her hospital room the night before the surgery. She didn't want to go on living if she wouldn't be able to continue getting on that bus.

Our brother, Ginger, died in November 2004, a few days before Thanksgiving. His death was sudden but not entirely unexpected. He'd long suffered from a seizure disorder and died in a cab pulling away from a hospital after checking himself out against medical advice.

Marilyn and Alex were my closest remaining relatives, and the only ones with whom I had a deep, long-lasting, loving relationship. Because Marilyn was seventy-five and Alex eighty-six, I had thought about what life would be like without them, but neither then had a serious health problem. They lived vibrant lives and were driving to a matinee movie with Alex's roller skates in the trunk when their car swerved into oncoming traffic on a busy, rain-slicked road.

They lived outside Philadelphia, and the trauma center where Alex had been taken was in Delaware. I quickly grabbed some clothing, aware that I might not be back home for a few days, and drove the two and a half hours from Northern Virginia to the trauma center, where I arrived around midnight, minutes after Alex was declared dead. During the trip, I played my collection of songs by Andrew McKnight so that I could hear a friend's voice as I drove alone.

One of his songs, "Good Things Matter," exemplified the way they lived.

Good things matter, no matter how small.

I got to hold Alex's hand before the body was removed.

In the days that followed, I learned that their car had swerved into oncoming traffic. The first car coming from the other direction clipped the right front of their vehicle enough to swing it so that the passenger side, where Alex sat, was in the direct path of the next car, which couldn't avoid plowing into it. The driver of that car, a clergyman, left his car to offer whatever help he could even though his arm had been broken by the impact.

Because the driver of the first car attended the funeral and identified himself to me, I was able to deliver a message I felt needed to be expressed. I planned to also reach out to the other driver to deliver the message. A bishop in the Anglican Church, he wasn't hard to find. With some anxiety about the conversation we would have, I decided to call rather than meet in person. "I'm sorry for your loss," he told me. "From everything I've heard, they were good people, and they're now in God's embrace."

I thanked him for leaving his car and going to their aid. "That was no problem," he replied. "My arm wasn't too bad. As soon as I saw your sister, though, I knew she was gone."

I went on: "I have a message I've wanted to convey to you and the other driver: There's one thing I know for a certainty.

If my sister could, she'd want to apologize for what you went through."

I'll never forget his reply. Most of us would answer as the other driver had, by saying there was no need for an apology, but the bishop, without hesitation, said, "I accept the apology."

With those four words, he accepted more than the apology. He accepted my need to express it, my feelings as real. It was a lesson for me in accepting the good others can offer without letting differences in theology or politics interfere.

It wasn't the phone on June 1, 2015. It was the doorbell at 8 a.m. that presaged the news of my son Thomas's death. Two deputy sheriffs at my door—a man and a woman—asked if they could come in. I had watched videos urging viewers never to let the cops into their home, but I didn't hesitate. The man said he had bad news.

"Your son has died."

Carol and I had two sons. Neither lived at home and, to our knowledge, neither was suicidal or taking potentially lethal drugs. I realized later that this deputy sheriff must have failed to take adequate notes during the "notifications" class in his training. I had to ask, "Which one?"

He seemed to recognize he had erred in not using the name. "Thomas."

"How did he die? Was it suicide?"

"He fell off a skateboard and hit his head. The accident investigator in Charlottesville has the details. I'll give you his phone number, but he won't be in until 10 a.m."

"Would you wait here while I break the news to my wife and bring her downstairs?"

Carol said later that when I entered the bedroom, I was so pale that she thought I was having a heart attack, so she was confused when I told *her* to sit down. Later, when she explained that to me, I was surprised that my shock was so visible. In sudden traumas, I go into autopilot. Because my experiences have taught me how, I immediately start handling the details. Knowing that strong emotions lie ahead for me, I focus first on handling *stuff* and doing my best to support others in their grief.

In this case, my primary concern was Carol. Thomas was her birth son, whom I had adopted. Her connection to him had been much stronger than mine. I was aware, too, that our other son, Carl, who lived in Richmond, Virginia, would need to be brought into our circle of grief.

Carol couldn't make it all the way down the stairs but collapsed into a sitting position close enough to talk with the deputies. Once she had learned whatever they could tell her, they left, and we began running on a sort of grief hamster wheel—exactly the sort of role I am trained for. Carol was pleased to let me do most of the running while sharing the decision-making.

During the rest of that day, we did the following:

- Decided to make the five-hour round-trip drive to Richmond so we could break the news to Carl in person. I called him first and couldn't convince him that it was just a casual visit, so he knew something was up.
- Notified only one or two people and asked them to keep the information to themselves until we could tell Carl in person and we could be ready for calls, messages, and visitors.
- Talked with the accident investigator by phone and learned more details. He explained that Thomas died at

2 a.m., skating down a steep hill without a helmet, and that Thomas's body couldn't be released until the coroner agreed that the death was accidental.

- Contacted a local funeral home to learn about the procedures that would be involved in transporting his body and having it cremated.
- Broke the news to Carl, who was heartbroken. Despite the eight-year age difference between them, they had been buddies. Carl decided to drive to our home himself, so Carol and I were alone again for the return leg.
- Began discussing memorial services and lining up ministers on the ride home.
- Notified the rest of the world after we returned home, first via phone for those who needed to get the news directly from us and later by Facebook.

Because of the time Carol and I had to process the loss alone and without interruption that first day, we were better able to face together the continuing hamster wheel of grief over the next few weeks. That week, we had a sort of one-day *shiva* or wake, basically an open house for friends and relatives; we spoke with Thomas's friends in Charlottesville and spent Friday night bar-hopping with them as Thomas liked to do; we met in person with the accident investigator, who gave us Thomas's wallet, cell phone, and skateboard; we held a memorial service in that city for his friends there and planned another one near our home, where Thomas grew up; we collected Thomas's belongings and claimed his truck; we held a brief viewing for the five or six closest family members and had his body cremated; we opened a slew of sympathy cards; and much more.

I mention these details because the sudden, unexpected loss of a young loved one is more than an example of impermanence. It sets off a tsunami of events as it challenges the fundamental Buddhist teaching that we all suffer, get old, and die. Some of us don't have the opportunity to get old.

As Carol and I drove home that first day—June 1, 2015—we were able to absorb something else together. Thomas had long been a heavy drinker. He loved spending his weekends and some evenings in bars. He had been skateboarding home from drinking with friends. Later that week, we learned that he had been drinking all day and passed out at home around 4 p.m., then got up and went out again.

His death was clearly accidental. He was alone on his skateboard. The coroner didn't need a postmortem to establish the cause or manner of death, so that it wouldn't go into the statistics as alcohol-related. It did, however, reinforce my commitment to Buddhism's Fifth Precept. Millions of alcohol-related deaths like Thomas's don't go into the statistics as such.

CHAPTER 20

SPIRITUAL INTERLUDE—FINDING REFUGE IN COMMUNITY

Ven. Ananda said to the Blessed One, "This is half of the holy life, lord: admirable friendship, admirable companionship, admirable camaraderie."

"Don't say that, Ananda. Don't say that. Admirable friendship, admirable companionship, admirable camaraderie is actually the whole of the holy life."

That quotation from the Upaddha Sutta applies in some degree to any spiritual life. The Buddha may have been slightly hyperbolic in telling Ananda, his cousin and attendant, that healthy friendships are "the whole of the holy life," but he knew how to make a point. They matter a lot.

That's especially clear in a religion like Buddhism with no god issuing commandments, but even in religions with a sovereign creator-god, lay spiritual friends are go-to guides.

Christians meet in small-group fellowships: Bible-study groups, charismatic prayer groups, service organizations, youth ministries.

Jews form *chavurah* fellowship circles, meet in study groups, and join together for both charitable outreach and congregational support.

Muslims gather in *halaqas* (study circles) and gatherings for Quran study, remembrance, and mutual support.

Lay groups organize charitable initiatives and support systems for youth, women, and converts.

The closest thing Buddhism has to a creed is the simple Refuge Prayer:

I take refuge in the Buddha.

I take refuge in the dharma.

I take refuge in the sangha.

"Buddha" here refers to the man who lived 2,600 years ago, to all Buddhas of all time, and to the Buddhahood within each of us. "Dharma" means both what the Buddha taught and how the world works. "Sangha" is the spiritual community. With no baptism, confirmation, or conversion process in Buddhism, reciting the Refuge Prayer with sincerity is considered sufficient to consider oneself a Buddhist.

So finding a home in a *sangha* is as important in Buddhism as relying on the teacher and the teachings. When our son Thomas died, Carol and I participated actively in our Unitarian Universalist Church community and even hosted a weekly Buddhist meditation group at our home. Church members organized a brigade to bring us meals daily, and the weekly meditation group grew in numbers of members and the size of its heart.

After Carol and I both began a path in Vajrayana Buddhism with Lama Surya Das, we joined a sangha that meets daily via

Zoom with members throughout the United States. That sort of regular community support has been a core part of our spiritual growth.

Only 1 percent of North Americans identify as Buddhists, so we often depend on Zoom. Distance can be measured in miles or in heartbeats.

CHAPTER 21

JOE'S REVELATION AND MOISHE'S GIFT

With Marilyn gone, I had no one to approach with questions about the family history. She had been my go-to, and every family needs one. I didn't think I knew enough to be a reliable source for my children and nieces and nephews, but I started work on a family tree. At least I'd record the little I knew in a lasting record. I joined ancestry.com and made it my canvas. Of course, it would take a reincarnation of Einstein to create a family tree that would make sense for my family.

Because my father was my mother's uncle and my mother was my father's niece, no two-dimensional tree could make all the necessary connections. I'm simultaneously:

- The son of Jack and grandson of Shalom, with Morris as an uncle.
- The son of Fannie and grandson of Morris, with Shalom as a great-grandfather.

I'll leave it at that, but similar two-level reasoning applies to everyone else in my family. I did my best, but my ancestry.com family tree is inevitably sloppy.

When ancestry.com offered a genetic profile at a reasonable cost, I sent for the kit, spit into the tube, and was curious about what I'd learn. The first surprise was a cousin once removed named Karen Kaplan, the granddaughter of one of my father's (full) brothers. Discovering a new relative was great, and she came with a bonus—more skill and diligence as a researcher than I had.

She led the way in making two discoveries. I think Moishe Kantorowitz came first, but I start here with Joe Soll. In the genetic matches ancestry.com showed us, his name appeared as a close cousin to both Karen and me, but we had never heard of him and couldn't find a relative who had. It took a while, but here's what we eventually learned:

Joe can't be sure, but most likely he was born in 1939 in or around New York City. He was adopted by a lawyer and the lawyer's wife and grew up in Nyack, New York—and was told that his parents had been killed in an automobile accident. His adoptive parents later had a daughter and a son the old-fashioned way.

Joe became a successful broadcast engineer, but he was deeply neurotic about having been adopted. He hated to mention adoption or think about it. But one day in 1982, his adoption came up in conversation with his sister, who told him for the first time that the story of an automobile accident was a lie. In his early forties, Joe then went into a terrible spin, with a fierce need to learn who his natural mother was.

He learned that the story was more troubling than he imagined. His father had bought him from a criminal "baby broker" named Bessie Bernard, who has since become notorious in the adoption community. She had a forty-year career, punctuated by one jail sentence, of obtaining and selling babies, and always obscuring their past.

Joe turned his trauma into wisdom and compassion by joining the adoption community, going back to school for a master's in social work, and becoming a psychotherapist specializing in what he calls "adoption healing."

Despite having grown up never mentioning "adoption," he has written adoption healing books and co-founded Adoption Crossroads, an international, nonprofit organization consisting of more than 470 adoption agencies, mental health institutions, and adoption search and support groups in eight countries, representing more than half a million individuals whose lives have been affected by adoption. He has organized and coordinated international mental health conferences on adoption and has served as an expert witness in adoption-related cases.

Oh, and three times he walked from New York City to Washington, DC, to support open adoption records.

But despite helping thousands to find their natural mothers, Joe, who was seventy-four when Karen and I met him, despaired of ever finding his. Using the few details that Joe was able to provide, Karen and I came up with a most likely candidate to have been Joe's mother. Ruth was my cousin and the mother of Bobby, the reason I was born. She was twenty-two or twenty-three, unmarried, and living with her mother and little sister in a crowded apartment in the New York City borough of Queens in the closing years of the Great Depression.

Ruthie would get married about five years later and gave birth to Bobby in 1945. I remember one conversation with her that left me with the impression that there might have been another child in her past. Ruth died in 1987 at the age of seventy.

My first visit with Joe, in early 2014, coincided with the news he received that confirmed Ruth was indeed his mother. After thirty years of frustration and after helping thousands of others, Joe finally learned about his mother and for the first time met some blood relatives. He was ecstatic and began a practice he continues as I write this in November 2025. Every night, he sends a good-night email to his newfound cousins. It usually arrives in my inbox around 10 p.m.

When I returned home after that first visit with Joe, I found the gift card that Ruthie gave me on my bar mitzvah day, May 2, 1959. I could give Joe something his mother had held and signed almost fifty-five years earlier.

My cousin Ruth

Moishe Kantorowitz was born in 1923 in Shereshov, the shtetl that my father came from. The area was controlled at times by Poland and at times by Russia, but in the Jewish shtetls they spoke Yiddish, learned Hebrew as their written language, and identified as Jewish. My father had emigrated about two years before Moishe was born, and my mother's parents had emigrated from the area two decades earlier. In the 1920s, my father's brother and sister married Moishe's uncle and aunt. So Moishe and I were first cousins by marriage.

Moishe was seventeen when the Nazis occupied Shereshov in June 1941. He lived with his parents, an older sister, and three younger siblings; for almost two years, they led a nomadic, hungry, and horrific existence avoiding the Nazis and staying alive. Finally, though, in 1943, the time came when they knew the Nazis would be rounding them up the next day. They thought they were going to be marched out of town and shot, a fate they had seen so often. They didn't know yet about the death camps.

The night before the Nazis were scheduled to come for them, Moishe's mother, Esther-Beila, took him by the hand out to the porch of the home they were staying in and sent him off. He was the only one of the family with a chance of escaping the ghetto and joining the Resistance. Knowing that she and the rest of the family were about to die, she asked him to memorize the address of one of her two brothers living in the Bronx. Her instructions: "If, God willing, you survive, go tell them how we lived and how we perished."

Then she couldn't bring herself to hug him, but stood stoically and watched him go—the last they saw of each other.

His family was rounded up on schedule, packed into freight cars, and gassed at Auschwitz. Moishe managed to hide from the roundup just for one more day, and then he too was packed into a freight car and transported to Auschwitz. He never made it to the Resistance. But because of his age and vigor, when he got to Auschwitz, he was put to work instead of being killed immediately.

The work, the starvation, and the beatings were brutal, and several times over the next two years Moishe came close to death, yet he managed to live through five concentration camps and several death marches. When the war ended, Moishe weighed eighty pounds, but he was alive.

One of the very few Jewish survivors from Shereshov, he made his way to Canada, where he married, had three children and five grandchildren. Before Moishe died in 2008 at the age of eighty-five, he wrote down everything he could remember not only about his own ordeal but about *everyone* from Shereshov. And he had a phenomenal memory for detail. He called his book *My Mother's Bequest*. It's a PDF file of 671 pages, available for free to anyone who wants to learn what happened to their relatives in Shereshov. He did what Esther-Beila had asked him to do—and much more. He told the story for his uncle and for everyone else who wanted to know about their own lost relatives.

My newfound cousin Karen found that book for us. Esther-Beila's bequest, and Moishe's as well, had made its way to us. Our relative by marriage, whom we'd never met, Moishe had supplied the details of the lives and brutal deaths of the uncles and aunts and cousins we never thought we'd know much about. Through Moishe's own saga, we also learned what it's like for a family to spend two years on the run from genocidal pursuers.

I've watched videos of Moishe—testimonies of a Holocaust survivor—but the account he wrote in Yiddish and had translated for people like Karen and me goes much further in conveying the horror of those years.

As Joe did, Moishe transformed his trauma into compassion and healing. Moishe's descendants live on, mostly in Canada, and the record he made of the Holocaust's effect on all the residents of a small Nazi-occupied Jewish community became a gift to their descendants, including my entire extended family.

CHAPTER 22

SPIRITUAL INTERLUDE—LOOKING BACK

January 1995 began as January 1990 had—with me in a vortex of life events that might appear in a *Reader's Digest* or *Psychology Today* list of top-ten life stressors. You know the type of article. It often comes with a quiz:

- Have you lost a respected loved one in the past year?
- Have you changed your residence in the past year?
- More than once?
- Have you lost your job?
- Are you adjusting to new roles in your professional or family life?
- Are you still working out the kinks in your marriage?
- Is your immediate family adjusting to a new member of the household?

This time was awful again, but I was better able, both psychologically and spiritually, to meet it. The climb from the chasm into which I had fallen on November 3, 1984, sitting on the floor listening to "Hey Jude," had been hampered by the Mother of All Midlife Crises.

Writing a spiritual memoir forces one to rethink the past, looking for paths and turning points. Because my Tibetan dharma name translates to "Fearless Lotus" and since Thich Nhat Hanh often used the metaphor of the lotus needing the mud to grow from, I looked up the actual process.

The seed first germinates in the darkness of pond sediment, sending down roots that anchor into the mud; this nutrient-rich but lightless beginning is essential. A shoot emerges upward, growing through the murky water in a determined vertical climb. The stem contains air channels that allow it to breathe even while submerged, and it's coated with a waxy substance that repels water and dirt.

As the stem pushes upward, it remains flexible enough to navigate obstacles but strong enough to maintain its upward trajectory.

When it finally breaks the surface, the bud emerges tightly closed, then gradually unfolds over several days into that pristine flower—completely clean despite its muddy origins, thanks to that remarkable hydrophobic coating that causes water and dirt to simply roll off.

The lotus never tries to avoid the mud or rush past the dark water. It draws nourishment from the very conditions that seem most difficult, transforms that sustenance during its patient ascent, and finally opens into something beautiful precisely because of—not in spite of—where it began.

The turning point for me, when I became both strong and flexible enough to maintain my upward trajectory, was hearing these words over a pay phone receiver alongside the highway from Philadelphia:

If he was my husband, he wouldn't have died of heart disease . . . I would have killed him first.

That voice happened to come from a psychiatrist, but one talking to a suitor over the phone who made a crack she probably never would make to a patient. In addition to my dropping the idea of suicide, selling the gun, marrying Carol, adopting Thomas, and giving life to Carl, here's what was going on spiritually:

- I metabolized my past traumas. Hitting bottom and turning toward the light enabled me to learn from those actions and then to understand better that suffering is impermanent.
- I began therapy with a gifted and mature psychiatrist named Steve Baker, who was a better match for me than any previous therapist.
- I intensified my mindfulness-based Buddhist practice. The walk-in closet in the master bedroom of our new home would become my meditation sanctuary.

The most important learning I incorporated into my being, which has helped me through every crisis since, came from the refuge I found from debt collectors in 1989 and 1990. I'll express it in more Buddhist language later, but I found it eloquently expressed as I read the book I mentioned in the Introduction by a Roman Catholic professor of spiritual formation.

In his memoir about recovering from much different traumas than mine, *Cradled in the Arms of Compassion*, Frank Rogers Jr. writes the following about a teaching he absorbed from one of his college professors:

Dr. [James Earl] Massey rocked my world with the possibility that God can be found within the hearth of my own soul, and that, having never left, God is

> *already there waiting for me to come back home to myself.*

In mindfulness-based Buddhist practice, I will say that this way:

> *I can always find refuge in the present moment. When I live here and now, nothing can harm me. If my mind wanders to worries about the past or future, I can bring it home to the shelter of now.*

In Vajrayana (Tibetan) Buddhism, I will add:

> *When I rest without distraction in pure awareness, with thoughts coming and going like clouds in the sky, I am experiencing the true nature of mind, the Buddha Nature.*

You may disagree that those statements all say the same thing. You may be certain that an authentic state of grace can't be reached without belief in a creator sovereign god. Or you may be certain that belief in that sort of god is a distraction that pulls one away from understanding the true nature of the world.

Whatever your belief system, what leads to awakening is a spiritual process.

The decade from 1995 to 2005 included two years of my sending out hundreds of résumés, two years of a steady job, five years of moderately successful freelance and consulting work, and a spectacular business failure before another business lasted until my retirement at the end of 2015. I joked then that I wasn't retiring—I was beginning a permanent spiritual sabbatical.

The sabbatical morphed into another full-time (not-for-profit?) business in 2024, doing some spiritual writing and publishing that I hoped would relieve my suffering. It also led, with a few more challenges along the way, to my full awakening to a life of joy.

Just as traumas are cumulative, so are the lessons learned from them—the gifts they give us. My path to that life of joy began when I was nineteen and started two years of psychotherapy. The phrase "the body doesn't forget" didn't come into use until the 1990s, but my body confirmed two themes that emerged during that course of therapy:

- My mother wanted me not to exist.
- My mother didn't show any affection toward me.

The psychiatrist Bernard Blum was my first therapist, who diagnosed me as suffering what then was called "reactive depression." Duh! The antidepressant he prescribed—before the more modern ones were available—did its job, along with Dr. Blum's therapy. Three times a week, then twice a week, and then once a week, I'd lie on a couch—yes, literally—with a chair arranged to block my view of him at his desk. As I remember it, the fifty-minute sessions consisted of me free-associating and him voicing occasional comments and questions. Typical Freudian therapy.

Fannie paid for my therapy. I was working as a "delicatessen man" at a Jewish deli—slicing lox, corned beef, tongue, salami—and paying my own tuition at Temple University, so I couldn't afford the therapy and didn't understand how my mother did. I learned later that Marilyn and Alex were sending her monthly checks, which she refused to use for herself. I had been giving her part of my earnings, which she also refused to use. She deposited everything she received, other than Social Security checks and what she made babysitting, in a savings account intended for my future, so I assume now that the money came from there.

Mom expressed her love by protecting me from physical harm and worrying about my health. When I was younger—up to the time of my father's first heart attack—she was a walking caricature of the overprotective mother. She worried if I got too close to an electric socket, or if I didn't thoroughly dry my hands before touching a light switch, or if I came near any body of water higher than my ankles, and even if it was a running stream of any depth, I wasn't allowed near it because of polio risk.

When I mentioned that overprotectiveness to Dr. Blum, I didn't think of it as significant, but he said, "To quote Shakespeare: 'The lady doth protest too much, methinks.'"

That surprised—and shocked—me. The shock came because I didn't think he would ever be that direct. He was implying that my mother wanted me dead. But after months—maybe years—I realized he was right.

In 1945, when Jack and Fannie made their fateful, condomless trip to New York, they were living in a small South Philadelphia row house with Ginger, age fourteen; and Marilyn, ten; plus Bubbe, who was seventy; Fannie's brother Harry and sister-in-law Dorothy; and their two children, Martin, thirteen, and Jay, five. Dorothy had a severe psychiatric illness, but all they understood then was that she'd fly into rages and severely beat Martin for offenses as small as not finishing his meal. The house was crowded, noisy, and violent, so the last thing Fannie wanted was a newborn baby.

I suspect that whatever passion led to me was a blip in Fannie's developing frigidity, which became more overt after they moved into the house on F Street in late 1946. In this bigger house, Fannie began sleeping on the living room sofa.

No statistics exist on the prevalence of infanticide in 1946 in the United States. An abortion for a poor Jewish woman living in a South Philadelphia row house would have been close to impossible, and frightening. The annual rate of deaths from illegal abortions in the United States in that era was more than a thousand.

According to a DePaul University study, local law enforcement officials were reluctant to prosecute women for that crime in those days, especially if they were married. I'm aware of one instance from the early 1950s that appears to have been a mother using a pillow to smother a newborn and then simply reporting the unexplained death. What leads me to near-certainty that my mother considered that solution, and even began to try it out on me, is the modern concept of "the body doesn't forget."

I have always had a fear of smothering—a fear of being buried under something, unable to breathe. It took me years after my first sexual experiences before I could allow the woman to be on top, and I was quick to dislodge her afterward. I'm uncomfortable being hugged too tightly or too long.

Another incident from that first period of psychotherapy with Dr. Blum was the surfacing of my first memory. I think I was around four when I would wake up every morning in the same state. Morning after morning, before I opened my eyes, I felt in my mouth the most satisfying substance imaginable, if only I could get my teeth into it. But there was some mysterious force keeping my teeth from fully making contact with it.

As I describe that now, the general idea of what was going on is obvious. But when I was nineteen or twenty, I was mystified by the memory. When I described it to my sister, she said, "Oh, that's easy to understand. Mom had trouble nursing you and wore nipple guards."

That explains my oral fixation. I was overweight for much of my life because the satisfaction of the food in my mouth carries more importance than the fullness of my stomach. I smoked and then vaped. I still do. I sucked wintergreen Life

Savers as a kid and switched to Ricola lemon-mint lozenges as a more affluent adult. Recently, I started chewing gum.

But more important than the oral fixation is that my mother didn't want me and lacked affection for me. The physical barrier of the nipple guards transformed into the invisible barrier that kept her from hugging me, which shows up as an inch or two of space in family photos.

The body doesn't forget.

> *Aujourd'hui, maman est morte. Ou peut-être hier, je ne sais pas.*

That's how Camus wrote the famous first line of his novel *The Stranger.*

> *Mother died today. Or yesterday maybe, I don't know.*

When I heard or read as a teenager that a man named Albert Camus had written a book about a main character put on trial for not loving his mother, I had to read it. Because the novel deals with absurdity, existentialism, and detachment—using Meursault's indifferent but slightly caring attitude toward his mother as a device—I found it disappointing. To refresh my memory as I wrote this passage, I asked the AI platform Claude Sonnet 4.5 to describe Meursault's attitude. Here's part of the response:

> *His attitude isn't one of active dislike or resentment—it's more profound than that. It's an absence of the emotional responses society expects. He seems to have cared for her in a practical sense (he had arranged for her care at the home), but he*

> *lacks the conventional grief, sentimentality, or even the pretense of such feelings that others display.*

Once I grew out of my teenage resentment, that became my attitude. I was attentive and present for my mother's death, and I delivered a eulogy at her funeral, expatiating on her humor and what she had to teach us about getting on the bus. I cared about her well-being, as she had cared for mine, but I also mirrored her lack of more-overt forms of affection toward me. If I were ever put on trial for not loving my mother, I'd plead self-defense.

CHAPTER 23

EARLY ADOPTER OF ANOTHER TRAUMA

Is there a word for being a negative pioneer? Just as I was early to be burned by an internet romance, I was canceled before that word came into common use—canceled by my chosen religious institution.

The Unitarian Universalism that I became part of in the mid-1980s was about members supporting each other in our honest respective searches for truth and meaning in life. I'm thankful that it encouraged my growth in Buddhism. UUism had a history of supporting social action while welcoming everyone, even if they didn't choose to go out marching. Petitions and signs were kept separate from what went on in the sanctuary.

UUism supported my growth in Buddhism, and Buddhism informed my activity in UUism. As a Unitarian Universalist, I:

- Served as president of one congregation and vice president of another

- Served as president and as director of an annual intentional community
- Served on the board of a district
- Founded a listserv for lay worship leaders to support each other
- Attended three annual General Assemblies, one as my congregation's delegate
- Wrote and delivered scores of sermons, many on aspects of Buddhism
- Was granted the status of a community minister
- Wrote a prayer called "We Thank Them All" that was accepted into the WorshipWeb Library of materials for members to use during services and was included in several published collections

As a prelude to how things turned sour in 2017, step back with me to 1999 or 2000. As a member of the Unitarian Universalist Association's Joseph Priestley District Board, I was required to attend one of the new antiracism programs being proudly rolled out. I chose one in Philadelphia and drove up from Northern Virginia, where Carol and I lived. UUism was a central part of our life together.

This antiracism was supposed to be new and improved over the old idea of equal rights. The training started with presentations about how whites have advantages over blacks. While I avoid gross generalizations, I accept that—on average and in many situations, all other things being equal—whites *are* likely to be treated better than blacks. But I drew the line when the trainers coaxed me to say four words: *I benefit from racism.*

The class came to a standstill and wouldn't proceed until I said those words, but my deep moral and spiritual beliefs wouldn't let me say them. I'll admit to having some relative advantages because of racism, but the word "relative" is the key. Racism brings us all down. It is not an issue owned exclusively by people of color; racism damages the entire culture. As the Reverend Martin Luther King Jr. said, "We may have all come on different ships, but we're in the same boat now."

My classmates joined the teachers in trying to get me to say those four words: *I benefit from racism.* One of them was a black man living in a predominantly white middle-class neighborhood whose son sometimes got hassled by the police when he went home for a visit. I tried to explain that I don't *benefit* from the hassling of his son, but no one wanted to hear it, so I became the class dunce.

I began withdrawing from UU leadership roles, except as part of worship services.

Shortly after Thomas's death, I dove deeper into spiritual practice and began blogging regularly. My blog eventually became *Melting-Pot Dharma*, which was mainly about Buddhism but occasionally touched on UUism. On April 12, 2017, I wrote a post about a shakeup in the UUA's leadership that had the markings of a coup. Here's the critical part of that piece:

> *In a nutshell (pun not intended but appreciated now that I see it), a coup has disrupted the democratic process.*
>
> *The demands of one UU faction have led to the resignation of the denomination's democratically elected president (three months before the natural end of his eight years in office), the resignations of the chief operating officer and a department head, and the decision by a parish minister to decline the leadership role to which he had been appointed.*
>
> *The denomination's annual General Assembly, at which a new president will be elected, is scheduled for June 21–25, and the new president takes*

> *office immediately. But the faction now in control is determined to get what it wants before then, so the Board of Trustees has appointed three interim co-presidents and charged them to give the faction what it wants before the new president is elected at the regularly scheduled General Assembly.*

I knew that some people would object to my post because of race. The issue that led to the resignations was the pace at which people of color were getting leadership jobs. Even though Peter Morales, the president who resigned, had a Spanish immigrant father and a mother of Mexican heritage, he was considered an obstacle.

I wasn't afraid of the criticism I expected to come, but—like so many others who have been canceled in various situations since—I had no idea how vicious and personal the response would be.

Something else I didn't understand was that, while my gripe was with the mostly white denominational figures who I believed had engineered the coup, the minority groups (the faction) that had been protesting what they saw as the president's too-slow approach felt my post was aimed at them.

Less than twenty-four hours after my post appeared, a woman named Leslie Mac, one of the founders of Black Lives of Unitarian Universalism, did a live eighteen-minute-long video feed on Facebook attacking me. Some quotations from the video about the blog post and me:

> *. . . white fragility and white centering . . . pissy language about being a Buddhist . . . fuckshit behavior . . . Your experience as a white man in the faith is what everyone is catering to . . . racist dog-whistle . . . white supremacist rhetoric . . . You have no morals . . . You're not going to be safe anymore . . .*

Before this video, I had never heard of Leslie Mac, and I'm sure she had never heard of me before my blog post the previous day. Unitarian Universalism was hardly aware of my *Melting-Pot Dharma* blog, which was better known in the Buddhist community. But Mac did some research on the county in which I live and mentioned three reported incidents of racist acts, declaring that I'm "cool" with them and see them as "the norm."

She even found what she called my "poem" posted on the Worship Web and read it in her vidcast:

We Thank Them All

Some came here looking for solace. Some came here and gave it to them.

Some came here seeking music. Some came here and gave it, joyfully.

Some came here seeking laughter. Some came here and created it.

Some came here seeking learning, growth. Some came here and provided it.

Some came here looking for a sense of security, a safe haven. Some came here and provided that.

Some came here seeking an escape from hectic lives. Some came here and enabled them to have it.

Some came here seeking the joy of community. Some came here and created that.

Some came here wanting to serve. Some came here and made it possible for them.

We thank them all.

Mac concluded the video by saying, "The words sound great, but it's a lie."

She decided that I meant those words only for white people and that I didn't want black people in my church. She inserted "white people" into my last line:

We thank all the white people. You don't mean we thank them all—at all.

The last part of her video stung me the most. Being repre sented with a prayer on the WorshipWeb was an honor, especially for a layperson, but now she had thrown mud on it. As for the rest of what she said, I was sure anyone watching it would realize that her video was an unwarranted ad hominem attack. My blog post was about the lack of a democratic process without mentioning or expressing an opinion on the organization's presidency or the racial makeup of the staff.

Boy, was I wrong!

Until then, it would be rare for one of my posts to get more than thirty-five views on a given day. After the Mac video, views of the post she responded to quickly climbed into the thousands. The negative responses started coming in—from friends, ministers, and UUA staff members—some very angry, some offering advice on how I should apologize. I remember especially one email from a UU minister who also practices Buddhism. He couldn't understand how I, calling myself a Buddhist, could have so blatantly broken my "covenant" with Leslie Mac.

Another minister wrote a blog post saying that the colonization of the Native American peoples was because of people like me. A couple of trolls started following me on social media and disputing anything I posted. I was threatened on Facebook and Twitter. One Twitter post about me read: "These white people won't understand until we turn the tables on them."

I wrote an apology for any harm my words had done, and I tried to explain my intent, but nothing helped. I hadn't understood until then how the "antiracism" movement had grown to dominate the dialogue about race, at least among the middle-class, educated, progressive, mostly white people who considered themselves UUs. One white UUA leader wrote a memo to all UUs declaring that "we swim in a sea of white supremacy."

While all that was a devastating shock to the values I had grown up with, I could live with it and still consider myself a UU until . . .

A month or two later, a friend texted me that she couldn't find my "We Thank Them All" on the WorshipWeb. I checked, and she was right. The prayer had been removed from the library, and my name had been removed from the index. After writing to the UUA to ask why, I received this reply:

> *May 16*
> *Hi Mel,*
>
> *Thanks for contacting us. Your email was forwarded to me, as I am the supervisor for WorshipWeb. Yes, you are correct, your pieces have been removed from the collection. We are always reviewing the WorshipWeb collection, and as I understand it your pieces had been there since before our current WorshipWeb Curator arrived.*
>
> *Your submissions were removed because your recent public comments made it difficult for these pieces to be interpreted in the way they had been before. As our Association struggles with the nature of whiteness' supremacy, we have to reexamine past assumptions, such as the assumption that a piece of writing can be interpreted independent of its source. Inclusion in the WorshipWeb collection as an author is, of course, always subject to the discretion of our editors. They felt (with my agreement) that these pieces and your voicing in them were not*

> *appropriate for WorshipWeb at this time, as we are committed to having hard and honest conversations about racial inequity in Unitarian Universalism.*
>
> *The editorial decisions on these pieces are final, though you are still free to submit additional pieces for consideration if you choose to do so.*
>
> *In faith,*
> *—Carey*
> *Carey McDonald | Outreach Director*

My prayer had been removed *not* because of its content but because its association with me was a stumbling block to "hard and honest conversations about racial inequity in Unitarian Universalism."

The faction devoted to giving UUism a creed after all—a political/social one—had apparently taken over the Unitarian Universalist Association. Fortunately, I was able to find community in Buddhism, and it took over as my religion as well as my spiritual home.

CHAPTER 24

SPIRITUAL INTERLUDE —RELIGIOUS TRAUMA

Spiritual trauma—psychological harm caused by religious or spiritual experiences—is real, widespread, and rarely discussed openly in spiritual communities. We're quick to talk about trauma healing through spiritual practice, but slower to acknowledge when spiritual practice itself becomes traumatic.

The psychologist Marlene Winell, who coined the term "Religious Trauma Syndrome," describes it as occurring when religious beliefs and practices cause significant mental distress and impairment.

It takes many forms. There's the obvious kind: clergy sexual abuse, financial exploitation, cult manipulation. These get attention because they're dramatic and clear-cut. But there's also a quieter, more insidious variety that's harder to name. It includes the teacher who uses shame to motivate practice. The sangha that enforces conformity through social pressure. The doctrine that convinces you your depression is just "bad karma" you need to meditate away. The practice community that pathologizes healthy boundaries as "ego." These leave marks too.

In the Vajrayana Buddhism I practice, respect for the teacher sometimes transforms into veneration, as though the teacher is a buddha walking among us. If the teacher does something that would appear inappropriate, it's being done for the student's enlightenment and should never be questioned. If a teacher has been accused of a misdeed, that should not be reported. Those misunderstandings of the core Buddhist teachings find expression too frequently.

Catholicism shares with Buddhism a culture that includes powerful patriarchs with total control over sequestered communities. I respect those traditions while remaining painfully aware that abuses have occurred and will always occur down through time.

Every spiritual tradition has its shadow side. The specific theology changes, but the pattern remains: spiritual authority wielded in ways that harm rather than heal.

What makes spiritual trauma particularly damaging is the way it hijacks our deepest search for meaning. We come to spiritual practice because we're suffering, because we're seeking something larger than ourselves, because we're trying to understand this difficult business of being human. We arrive vulnerable and hopeful. When that vulnerability gets exploited—or when the tradition simply fails to hold our pain with wisdom—the betrayal cuts more deeply than ordinary disappointment.

The symptoms look like other traumas: hypervigilance, shame, dissociation, difficulty trusting, self-hate, confusion about what's real. But spiritual trauma adds extra layers. Doubt about your own perception becomes doubt about your spiritual worthiness. Fear of authority figures becomes fear of faith itself. Anger at harmful teachers becomes doubt that you're capable of authentic practice.

Recovery requires something counterintuitive: *We need to grieve what happened while not abandoning the possibility of genuine spiritual life.* This isn't easy. Some people leave religion entirely, and that's sometimes necessary. Others find different teachers, different traditions, different approaches. Some return to their original path but with clearer boundaries and healthier skepticism.

What helps most is breaking the silence. Naming spiritual trauma for what it is. Recognizing that critical thinking and reverence are not opposites. Understanding that genuine teachers welcome questions, healthy communities allow dissent, and authentic practice never requires abandoning your basic dignity or denying your lived experience.

The path should liberate, not bind.

On my spiritual path as a teenager, I reacted to the rabbi's self-centered remarks, on top of my doubts about the faith, by rejecting Judaism. When, after Barry killed Eddie and Margaret, I found Unitarian Universalism, I came to terms with my Jewish roots and even led services honoring that religious tradition. My UU spiritual trauma came after I had gained wisdom from my life tragedies, secular learning, meditation, and religious practices. Rather than being a boulder blocking my path, the UU cancellation was a large rock that I made my way around.

The Buddha lived in an era when wandering ascetics offered teachings in return for offerings of sustenance. In the often-cited Kalama Sutta, residents of one region told the Buddha they were confused by the various doctrines they were taught. Which teachings should they believe?

He told them: "It is proper to doubt, to be uncertain." He advised them to ask themselves about any teaching:

Does it lead to "benefit or harm"? Does it foster "benefit and happiness"?

That teaching was given 2,600 years ago, but it's as ancient and current as the North Star.

CHAPTER 25

A JOYFUL SOUND FILLED THE ROOM

Carol didn't know she was rescuing me from suicide, but her day job is getting lives back on track. She's a psychiatrist. I don't know when I told her of the solid plan to kill myself that became fluid and then vapor during the early days of our lives together, but she has the experienced practitioner's ability to separate her profession from her home life.

I got used to fielding the inevitable questions about what it's like to be "psychoanalyzed" by my wife with this quip: "She's a psychiatrist who leaves her compassion at the office."

That wasn't true, of course, but giving her patients the one-pointed focus they're paying for leaves her yearning for a respite at home. Over time, though, as in any ongoing relationship, we learned the details of each other's lives. After the early years of ours, an insight came from four words she said: "You brought yourself up."

I hadn't seen my childhood and early adult years from that perspective. Those four words explain a lot. On the plus side, the observation emphasizes how self-regulated I became. It also highlights the vital role that Alice Johnson played. On the minus side, it casts a spotlight on what wasn't there—family structure, support, and parenting. Looking back, I understand why I fell so easily into relationships.

One thing that impressed Carol about me was how willing I was to take on Thomas. With Julie, I had taken on four young children whose father had just killed himself and a teenage stepdaughter who had been through sexual abuse and the death of the perpetrator. When Georgie and I moved into our first house together, her daughter spent her last year of high school with us and remained an important part of our lives.

With no conscious awareness of it, I actually longed for family life. I sometimes did the arithmetic to determine the theoretical age of the baby Susie and I had aborted.

Thomas's birth father died shortly after I entered his life and hadn't been present since he was a baby, so Thomas was glad to have a father. He wasn't ready to adjust to a new personality in his family, but he never wavered from knowing me as his dad.

With her outdated view of relationships, my mother thought I was infertile, once telling me: "Melvin, I don't think you'll ever have a child. You haven't had one yet even though you've been with so many women."

She didn't live long enough to learn that she was wrong.

From the start, Carol and I wanted to have another child, but a serious effort at tracking her menstrual cycle for about two years failed to result in a pregnancy. A consultation with a urologist indicated that, while I wouldn't win a gold medal in the Sperm Olympics, my gametes qualified for the team. We stopped trying but continued avoiding birth control.

As 1993 rolled into 1994, life otherwise was good. With my position at Mobil, where I'd worked for almost eighteen years, Carol might be able to cut down on her hours. To use a baseball term, I thought Mobil paid me well because of my talent as a "utility infielder." While not a star, I was more than competent in multiple positions and was well known throughout the organization. You could count on me for almost anything in a pinch.

I had fallen into one specialty—the important but nonglamorous job of managing the company's annual report. Requiring about a half year of full-time effort, the role required writing and editing skill, corporate diplomacy, budget administration, and enough familiarity with graphic design, photography, printing, and Generally Accepted Accounting Principles to hold substantive conversations with experts.

Mobil's president at the time, Lou Noto, was scheduled to take the chairmanship on March 1, 1994, and he had criticisms, or at least questions, about the annual reporting process. Some sort of document is legally required for a publicly traded corporation; but were the time, effort, and money required to make it slick and attractive justified by the return? I was appointed to lead a cross-functional study team to answer his question.

That put me in an incongruous position. I was chairing a committee of executives from various departments, all of whom stood on higher rungs of the corporate ladder than I did, which was likely to end up telling the incoming chair what he didn't want to hear. I suspect that we all came into the effort feeling that the report and the process of creating it didn't need a radical cutback, yet we started from a zero base:

- Could the steps of the accounting process be reduced?
- Should the report be only the legally required accounting with no front section for the general public?

- Did it need photos?
- Did the photos need to be in color?
- Did the report need an expensive, full-color cover?

We canvassed our foreign affiliates to learn how they used the annual report. We solicited opinions from the investment community. We studied the effect that individual investors have on the level and stability of the stock price, and we conducted focus groups of individual investors.

I drafted our report to Lou Noto, obtained comments from all the members of the team, revised the report, and got unanimous approval. The report would recommend ways to reduce some of the cost, but explained why the high-quality, public-facing content justified the expense.

Of course, it was my signature at the bottom of the report. It was returned to me from Lou with this comment written in pen at the top: "If this is the best they can come up with, I won't interfere."

That wasn't high praise, and both the team members and my public relations coworkers knew he wanted a more radical response, but it wasn't a rejection. As another study aimed at reducing the corporate staffing levels got under way, I believed that Lou's approval of me as the chair of the cross-functional team, his non-rejection of our report, and my value as a utility infielder with long experience meant that a continued role for me at Mobil was certain.

Carol's father, Carleton, was born in 1917 to a folksy but proud and domineering father and a stern mother. His father, Charles Johnston Harkrader, known as "Mr. Charlie," was a self-made entrepreneur in the city of Bristol, which straddles the Virginia–Tennessee border. He owned the *Bristol Herald Courier* newspaper, banks, a department store, an automobile tire store, and a radio station. He also served in the Virginia State Senate and its General Assembly. Carol's mother, Doris, was born on the Mediterranean island of Malta, just before her family moved to India, where her father, a Protestant Irish physician, served in the Royal Medical Corps. After surviving the Nazi bombings of London, she worked for the United Kingdom's Public Information Office, first in North Africa and then at the United Nations in New York City.

Carleton began his journalism career at his father's newspaper and won awards for the editorial page he ran before leaving to serve in the Second World War, after which he was a *Newsweek* correspondent in Europe and the Middle East. He returned to Bristol to run the *Herald Courier*. He met Doris, and she persuaded him to go to law school. After he was accepted at Yale, they married and began life together in New Haven, where Carol was born in December 1951. Carleton became a prominent Washington antitrust and regulatory lawyer, then moved from the Federal Trade Commission into private practice and co-founded the law firm of Wald, Harkrader & Rockefeller, which evolved into Wald, Harkrader & Ross.

That firm grew in size and influence in the 1970s and early '80s, but changes in the law business led to Carleton's retirement from active participation and the firm's eventual dissolution. When I met him in the early 1990s, he and Doris lived in a quiet house on a cul-de-sac in Great Falls, Virginia, that he had built with the help of their architect son. Soft-spoken, with an almost regal posture but a childlike sense of humor, Carleton did his best to live by the liberal principles formed in his decades of journalism and law. He was the kind of father figure I wanted.

By the time he and Doris entered my life, I had grown comfortable working with senior executives and traveling with them in limousines and corporate jets, but taking a role in their family was another new adjustment. Doris's family of origin was in a distant cloud somewhere across the Atlantic. The Harkrader clan established by Charlie, who had died in 1976, was dominant and ever-present—a strong culture that welcomed newcomers, but with caution.

Charlie had been suspicious that those who married into his family were after his money and the status that came along with his name. His five children married whom they chose to but didn't shed all of his caution. The next generation—Carol, her brother, their two sisters, plus their first cousins—shed the rest of the caution, yet a dividing line remained between Charlie's descendants and those who couldn't trace their bloodline back to him.

In my Pinsky family, spouses gained instant status as full members. This makes sense for a minority immigrant community. It didn't among the Harkraders. On the other hand, I was glad to gain a living and active father-in-law and mother-in-law as well as a position in a more-vibrant extended family, even if it came with an asterisk.

Eventually, I realized I had to erect a borderline of my own around the Pines. In our household, we decided what to feed our children, where to set the thermostat, and whether to lock the doors. The Harkraders treated each other's homes as communal spaces. Although Carol didn't notice that at first, she grew to understand my need to protect the integrity of our family unit.

In my role as the Mobil annual report project manager, I'd travel once a year, along with the company's design director, to oversee the printing process. In early 1994, that meant Boston. Before I left on my trip, I began to suspect that Carol was pregnant. I got her call while the design director and I were passengers in a car driven by the printing company owner, who was returning us to our Boston hotel after a press run. The lines on her test strip were both red, she told me. I was going to be a father, the old-fashioned way, for the first time.

Our purchase of a larger home in Reston, Virginia, and Carol's sale of her Leesburg house joined the to-be-expected stresses associated with her physical discomfort over the coming months. And there would be more. It was becoming clear that cancer was bringing Carleton's life to an end. At work, the big study leading to a reorganization had begun. Everyone had to reapply for a position. In my application, I said I'd be willing to take any position, even if it was two "salary grades" below my current one.

Because the sale of Carol's Leesburg house would close before the new Reston home was ready, Carol, Thomas, and I moved in with her parents for about two months.

Living under one roof yielded blessings with the bumps. We all got to know each other better, and the Pines got to share some of Carleton's last months with him. It was I who first expressed the idea of naming our child, whom we knew would be a boy, after Carleton, but without the last four letters. Most of us called Carol's father "Carl" anyway, and I preferred the shorter version, as I had with "Melvin." Carol agreed, and we broke the news to Carol's parents. The custom in Jewish families is to name children only after deceased relatives, so it delighted me to inform Carleton while he was still alive.

Before cell phones became common, hospitals rented "baby beepers" to expectant fathers. The pager sounded when it was time for Dad to call Mom. Carol's doctors had determined that a cesarean section would be needed and scheduled it in advance, so we thought we could have saved the cost of the beeper. But as I drove home from work on October 24—a week before the scheduled date—my beeper sounded. After pulling over at a bank of pay phones along the Dulles toll road, I called Carol, who told me this. "Luckily, it happened after my last patient. I sat down and felt liquid trickling down my legs. My water broke. I called the OB-GYN, and she told me she'd meet me at the hospital. Where are you? Please go home, tell Carl and the au pair that you'll be back late, and bring my bag to the hospital."

When I arrived at Reston Hospital, Carol was already in the operating room, but the staff got me washed and suited up to join her. I didn't have to tell them I was in a hurry. As I sat beside Carol's head, someone asked me if I wanted to see what was going on. When I said yes, he flopped down a corner of the two-foot-high screen that was blocking our view. Carol, sounding sedated, as she was, said, "I think I feel some tugging. Is something happening?"

I looked over the screen and saw the bloodied arms of the surgeon what seemed like six inches deep into Carol's abdomen, so I replied, "Yes. The doctor is getting started."

Once the OB-GYN had lifted Carl from her uterus and he was cleaned and examined, Carol and I got to hold him. It couldn't have been more than thirty minutes later before we were back in Carol's hospital room while Carl was being checked out further. She called her parents' house. Doris had gone out with Carol's sister, Elva, so Carleton, only twelve weeks from his death, answered the phone. Here's what I heard Carol say: "Hi, Dad. . . . Oh, pretty good for a woman who just had a baby."

The next sound filled the hospital room. The telephone receiver pressed to Carol's ear couldn't contain the sound of the grandfather's shout of joy.

We learned later that when Doris and Elva returned from their night out, a hand-lettered banner over the door read: CARL HAS BEEN BORN!

That Christmas, Carleton was able to hold Carl, dressed in a tiny Santa suit, on his lap before he died on January 6. A week later, the day of his memorial service was the day that, one by one, the members of Mobil's Public Affairs Department would learn their fate in the reorganization. The general manager had offered to delay my meeting with him by a day, but I asked him instead to schedule it for first thing in the morning so I could go to the service knowing what my next job would be.

Instead, he told me that my job would end after I finished getting that year's annual report to press in May. I felt stunned.

"You mean after May I have no job at all?"

"That's right."

"Can you tell me why I wasn't picked for one of the remaining jobs?"

"We've made the decision that we won't discuss individual cases."

I was immediately escorted to an office down the hall for my prearranged appointment with an outplacement consultant.

It hadn't been a reorganization. It had been a purge. The number of positions left unfilled in the new organization matched the number of employees who wanted jobs and were rejected. All without an opportunity to show what we could do when pointed in a new strategic direction.

My future earnings no longer ensured that Carol could begin reducing her patient load. So I attended the memorial service mourning my father-in-law and mourning my job, but proud to hold my three-month-old son on my shoulder.

CHAPTER 26

BEING THERE WHILE GETTING THERE

Losing a child, as Carol and I had done in 2015, leads to the dissolution of many marriages, but it strengthened ours. Carol and I reacted differently, of course, but the differences drew us closer. We respected and supported each other's distinctive forms of grief.

Mine involved taking a deeper dive into spirituality. I turned a blog I had launched earlier and done little with into *Melting-Pot Dharma,* and wrote an online post almost daily. My target audience was "the many who seek spiritual wholeness but don't feel at home with an imposed dogma." I wrote about Buddhist concepts as a lay practitioner and occasionally addressed issues in Unitarian Universalism.

On YouTube, I watched dozens of dharma talks from Buddhist teachers as well as sermons by both Unitarian Universalist and liberal Christian ministers. I stayed away from anything in the Tibetan tradition. While respecting the Dalai Lama and sympathizing with the Tibetans who'd had to flee the Chinese takeover, I felt that their version of Buddhism was too ritualistic for me.

When I noticed the name Lama Surya Das pop up as a subscriber to my *Melting-Pot Dharma*, I started checking him out. Although I knew he had a following in the Buddhist community, I had never before looked into him.

Over the thirty preceding years, perhaps a dozen men and women had contributed to my spiritual growth as a Buddhist, yet I considered Thich Nhat Hanh my primary teacher. He had an uncanny (some might say "God-given") talent for expressing Buddhist wisdom in language, metaphor, and humor that were all clear and meaningful for modern life. Here's an example from a talk I heard him give in New York City's Town Hall:

> *I don't have a telephone in the cottage where I live. But when I visit friends, I notice how tense they become when the phone rings. They jump up to answer it. So I thought maybe they could learn to treat the sound of the phone like the Bell of Mindfulness, inviting us to stop and breathe.*
>
> *On the first ring, they might stop, smile, and take a breath, thinking, "Listen to the sound of someone calling me." On the second ring: "I open my heart to this summons." On the third: "I will respond with loving-kindness and compassion." Then they will pick up the receiver in mindful presence.*
>
> *I understand that at first your friends will be impatient and annoyed, but eventually when they call, they'll think: "Now he's relaxing, breathing, and smiling." Then maybe they'll start doing it.*

His students called him *Thay*, Vietnamese for "teacher." During the Vietnam War, he refused to take sides. He had grown up in what during the war was South Vietnam, but when a reporter in the United States asked him where in Vietnam he was from, he said, "The middle." Thay and his fellow monks and nuns went into villages to rebuild homes, set up schools, and help whoever needed it. His refusal to take sides while working tirelessly for peace got him exiled from Vietnam for four decades, but he kept teaching wherever he went.

Martin Luther King Jr. nominated him for the Nobel Peace Prize, saying that giving it to Thay would show that peace comes from the people, not just politicians. Though he never won, his influence spread far beyond any award.

Without complicated jargon, Thay taught simple practices that anyone could do. Walking meditation? Just walk slowly and notice your feet touching the earth. Mindful eating? Actually taste your food. He'd refuse to let others wash his dishes unless they agreed to be fully present to the act of washing them.

His core teaching was basically this:

> *The present moment is all we have, and it contains everything we need. Stop running toward the future or dwelling in the past. Breathe in, breathe out, and notice you're alive.*

It sounds too simple, but he served as a walking embodiment of his teachings: *Peace is in every step.*

Thay's humanitarian works ranged from rescuing "boat people" fleeing after the war to holding retreats to help Western Vietnam veterans recover from their war trauma. He wrote more than one hundred books that have been published in English and founded both the Plum Village monastery and retreat center in France and the worldwide Order of Interbeing for lay and monastic followers of his teachings.

"Interbeing" is a core concept of Buddhism, especially as Thay taught it. He found the verb "to be" inadequate. Nothing can simply "be." It can only "interbe." He'd illustrate by asking you to hold a piece of paper and see in it the tree, the rain, the sunshine, the logger, the saw, the mill, and so on. I sometimes use a grace he wrote:

> *In this food, I clearly see the entire universe supporting my existence.*

Thay had a stroke in 2014 that left him unable to speak. He was, however, able to return to Vietnam to live out his remaining years. He died there in 2022 at age ninety-five.

In my three decades of regarding Thay as my teacher, I'd meditate daily for months at a time, then lapse for months, then resume. For one extended period, I'd spend an hour every morning meditating in a walk-in closet.

I attended teaching sessions and a weeklong retreat in Vermont with Thay, retreats led by one of his followers, meditation sessions and a retreat at a monastery founded by a Sri Lankan monk in the West Virginia woods; and I'd drop in now and then on local temples serving Asian immigrant communities. I read books by American Buddhists, such as Jack Kornfield. As a way to reinforce my learning, I led a weekly meditation group at the Reston church, then at one in Leesburg, then later at my home or someone else's.

But I was stuck on one thing. As I understood the teachings, we all have a Buddha within, and meditating is a way to get closer to it, along with compassionate and ethical living. But none of the Buddhist traditions I encountered depicted that "Buddha within" as being within reach. It was as though a mystical transformation called Enlightenment was lifetimes away.

That didn't conform to what my meditative experiences led me to believe. Perhaps it's presumptuous to call it Enlightenment with a capital "E," but getting closer to the "Buddha within" didn't need to be mysterious. We could get there here and now, I came to realize. I never heard Thay say that, but I did hear him say:

> *I know the address of the Kingdom of God. And the zip code, too. They are here and now.*

In the months following Thomas's death, I began to consider going away on a retreat. I had been running a local business and intensified my effort to sell the last piece of it, with the closing scheduled for December 31, 2015. As I looked into Lama Surya Das via Google and YouTube, I learned he was born Jeffrey Miller in 1950 to a Jewish family living in Brooklyn and then Long Island. The May 4, 1970, shooting deaths of four students at Kent State University was the tragedy that launched his spiritual quest.

After graduating from college in 1991, Jeffrey left the United States for what would become two decades of learning from Asian spiritual masters in India, Nepal, and a Buddhist retreat center in France. A sun-lover, he was given the name Surya Das ("servant of the sun"). "Lama" is the Tibetan honorific for "teacher."

I held in awe anyone who could leave one culture for a much different one in their early twenties, as my father had, especially one who left the comparative opulence of the New York City area for the severity of life in stark Asian subsistence communities.

I also learned that Surya Das was leading a retreat January 3 through 9 at the Garrison Institute in New York State. That's a five-hour drive from where I was living in Loudoun County, Virginia. I registered for it. In what seemed like an ideal start on what might become a new path on my spiritual journey, at the close of business on New Year's Eve, 2015, I picked up the payment for the business I had sold, then dropped the check in my bank's night depository. That act was my symbolic renunciation of mundane existence.

My new direction began early on the morning of Sunday, January 3, 2016, when I entered the Garrison Institute into Google Maps on my iPhone and began driving northeast.

I eventually grew to love silent retreats, but the instructions from the retreat manager after the evening meal that day at Garrison left me fearful. The "noble silence" was to begin immediately after her orientation talk and before we entered the meditation hall for our first session with Lama Surya. Did she really mean that we would not make even eye contact with each other until the Friday evening meal? And, since it had been just seven months since Thomas's death, what sort of mourning intensity might fill the void?

After some chanting, meditation, and a brief dharma talk, all led by Lama Surya, the welcoming session was over. We wouldn't be entirely silent for the week. We would chant, have the opportunity to ask questions after Lama Surya's talks, and even enter into a dialogue with him. That night, I didn't know quite what to make of him. Here was a man who had climbed up steep, snowy cliffs in the Himalayas to deliver meals to monks in caves, yet still spoke with a strong Brooklyn accent.

Later, with friends, I'd jokingly adopt an exaggerated New York accent to describe the experience: "C'mon, guys. Breathe in! Breathe out!"

I began to enjoy the quiet the next morning as, one by one, three dozen of us got our meals from the buffet, sat and ate, then took out plates to the kitchen, in silence and mostly without eye contact. I couldn't help being aware of the others, and I assumed some of them were aware of me. This wouldn't be as lonely as I thought it would.

Then a woman strode in, wearing colorful and disarrayed clothing and seeming to hum out loud or at least make muttering vocalizations. She made no visible effort to proceed slowly and mindfully or to refrain from making noise but quickly grabbed some food, dropped it into a pouch she had made in her skirt, and exited through the kitchen. She wore no coat this cold winter morning, so I wondered if she was eating alone in the woods.

I felt affronted by this intruder and also concerned about her, but I couldn't turn to another retreat participant and say something like *Did you see that woman? Was she a troubled homeless person sneaking in and stealing food? Do you think we should break the silence and alert someone?*

Instead, those questions buzzed around my head, or more accurately, swung from branch to branch in what we call the "monkey mind." When the dharma talk was about to begin in the meditation hall that afternoon, I saw her again and grew more affronted when she sat down in a row behind me. The intruder didn't leave—as I thought she would—when Lama Surya entered, took his seat, and began the talk. Nor did she cut back much on the vocalizations.

The woman, whom I'll call Sharon, had the audacity to ask a question. It sounded disjointed to me, but Surya gave her an answer and—surprise!—even knew her name. She must have been a regular at his retreats.

I learned a big lesson then. I needed some of the open-heartedness the teacher andother members of that sangha exhibited toward Sharon. To break through my negativity, I decided to practice co-meditation. While meditating, I'd invite her—or what I imagined her to be—into my mind to meditate with me. We'd co-meditate, and I began to feel what it was like to live with the need to make strange noises and wear startling clothing. The distance between us shrank, wordlessly. I felt it, and I learned on the last day of the retreat that she felt it, too.

She insisted on sitting next to me during the closing circle and even on carrying my luggage to my car.

That retreat covered the basics of Dzogchen, the tradition in which Lama Surya felt most comfortable teaching. I'll skip all but four details of Dzogchen:

1. It's pronounced with the "d" almost silent and the "g" hard: *dZOKchen*. Now you know how to pronounce it should the need arise.
2. It's one tradition in the Vajrayana School, which is often called Tibetan Buddhism.
3. The "view" of Dzogchen—the way practitioners perceive the world—is identical with the view of the Mahamudra tradition (which I'll mention again later) and somewhat similar to the views of other Vajrayana traditions.
4. The view of Dzogchen (and Mahamudra) is that the mind's intrinsic nature is pure awareness of the world as it truly is, undistorted by ego, clinging, and aversion. That's our Buddha Nature, and we can both reach it and learn to rest in it within one lifetime.

In Dzogchen, one begins and ends with the view. Lama Surya talked about "being there while getting there," swooping from above while climbing from below. I was to begin by learning the view cognitively and then reaching it experientially, mainly through meditation.

In other words, Lama Surya was both confirming my perception that Buddha Nature is closer than I had been led to believe and presenting a route to reach it. I had many questions for him during that first retreat. He told me years later that he knew from the first one that I was "learned." It was on Monday, the first full day. In the Q&A after his dharma talk, we had an exchange something like this:

Lama Surya, how close are you to the Buddha within?

How close are you?

Well, every tradition in Buddhism acknowledges that we have a Buddha within, but no one else has ever emphasized it. My own meditation has led me to believe I'm not far from it.

Congratulations. It's the same for me.

Two days later, I wrote him a note saying he was now my teacher. On Friday, I took refuge and the Bodhisattva Vow with him—an important ceremony in Vajrayana Buddhism. Decades earlier, I had gone through a similar ceremony and received a Vietnamese dharma name that translates to "Nectar of Compassion." The Tibetan dharma name that Lama Surya gave me is Urgyen Jigme, which translates to Fearless Lotus.

CHAPTER 27

EMPOWERMENT

During one of Lama Surya's retreats that I attended over the next five years, he answered a question by recommending one of his books, then decided that someone else's book said it better. I appreciate Surya's openness, and that of other teachers I've met. That trait seems to me more common—although not universal—in Buddhism than in other faiths. The Buddha taught nonattachment to views and ego.

Over those five years with Lama Surya, I felt that I had learned what I could from him and began exploring other Vajrayana teachers. Surya had gotten me over my resistance to Tibetan rituals. I'm still not a fan of those that are remnants of folk superstitions. I don't believe that if only I could circumambulate the 21,000-foot-high Mount Kailash 108 times, I'd be guaranteed enlightenment or entry into a pure land at death. But I do see how both chanting and ritual enhance my practice and perhaps connect with ancient sacred rhythms.

When I told Lama Surya that I had done a virtual retreat with Mingyur Rinpoche, he said he was glad I was getting to know him. He didn't add that he had known the *rinpoche* as a six-year-old child. That's because he and other Westerners who had gone to Southeast Asia to learn Buddhism in the early 1980s had studied with Mingyur's father, Tulku Urgyen Rinpoche. Before returning to Mingyur, here's a word about COVID and a brief spiritual crisis.

On March 11, 2020, the World Health Organization declared that COVID-19 was a pandemic. I had been attending a couple of retreats a year, almost all of them led by Lama Surya Das, but COVID meant no more in-person retreats at least until the pandemic was over, and that day didn't come until May 5, 2023. Carol and I had attended Lama Surya's last retreat before COVID, in October 2019, at the beautiful Serra Retreat in Malibu, California.

Lama Surya continued to lead a Meditation Town Hall on Sunday mornings via Zoom, which we regularly attended, and eventually Carol and I began meeting daily with a nationwide Zoom sangha of his students and others. That sangha especially helped us keep our practice going.

We had learned in 2017 that sexual accusations against Surya in 2008 had led to the resignation of his board and a sharp decline in his following, from which he never recovered. But as far as we were concerned, that was in the past, we saw nothing troublesome about his behavior, and we liked learning from him and being part of his community.

A July 30, 2020, article in the Religion News Service was the first published account of the scandal. The article portrayed the accusations as more serious than the stories we had heard and his reported response as less than admirable, but again this was all hearsay about what had happened a dozen years earlier, and we made the decision to remain his students. I even took a role publicly assisting him in some of the weekly town halls.

In October 2023, we attended his first post-COVID retreat, again at the Serra center. It was great being back with him and the community. But then the next retreat he scheduled, on the East Coast, was canceled at the last minute "for reasons beyond our control." A talk he was scheduled to give in Chicago was also canceled at the last minute, as was another retreat scheduled at a new location on the East Coast. In 2024, Lama Surya announced what he called his "rewirement" at the end of the year, with no prospect for more in-person retreats or teachings.

His lack of a public explanation to his followers put me into a brief spiritual crisis. I had—and still have—no idea if the accusations of misconduct are true. My speculation is that pressure from somewhere led venues to cancel his appearances, but I have no firsthand knowledge of that. What I do know for sure is that Lama Surya has not given a public explanation for the cancellations and "rewirement." Except as quoted in the Religion News Service article, he has not publicly acknowledged or responded to the allegations.

My spiritual crisis consisted of how to handle my discomfort. Although I'll always be grateful for his showing me the path to Vajrayana, I needed to make some sort of a break. If I no longer wanted to work with him on Sunday mornings, how could he still be my teacher? I call my spiritual crisis "brief" because Surya and I eventually exchanged emails in October 2024 and parted ways as friends.

Mingyur Rinpoche was born in 1975 into what could be considered Tibetan Buddhist royalty. His father, Tulku Urgyen, was one of the most revered Dzogchen masters of the twentieth century. Other masters often went to him for instruction. His hermitage at Nagi Gompa, perched on a ridge above Kathmandu

Valley, became a pilgrimage site for serious practitioners from around the world.

When Mingyur was recognized as a *tulku*—the rebirth of a Buddhist master—at a young age, it confirmed what his family lineage already suggested: He was destined for spiritual greatness. His brothers were also recognized tulkus and would become important teachers. But despite this spiritual pedigree, Mingyur was an anxious, panic-stricken kid. He often tells of his debilitating childhood panic attacks and his struggle to overcome them. He didn't at first believe his father's advice that meditation would help, but eventually it did, and he explains how he began to work directly with his anxiety. That's one way that he reveals he's not teaching from some untouchable mountaintop even though, in one sense, he is.

Or he was, until he spent four and a half years living anonymously in caves and on the streets of India and Nepal. In Vajrayana, three-year retreats in monasteries or retreat centers have been standard for serious practitioners and teachers, and Mingyur had taken one as a teenager. In his mid-thirties, as the abbot of one monastery and overseer of another, he was due for another, but he had a secret: He didn't need more time in a monastery. This retreat would be living on the streets. In his book *In Love with the World*, he writes:

> *I had set my sights on following the ancient tradition of sadhus, the wandering Hindu ascetics who give up all their belongings to live free of worldly concerns. The earliest heroes of my own Tibetan Kagyu lineage had followed in the footsteps of their Hindu predecessors, taking shelter in caves and forest groves. I would die to my life as a privileged tulku—a recognized incarnation of a spiritual adept. I would discard the mantle*

> *of being the youngest son of Tulku Urgyen Rinpoche, the esteemed meditation master. I would live without attendants and administrators and would exchange the protections granted by my role as abbot and lineage holder for the anonymity that I had never known but had long yearned for.*

Rinpoche spent months preparing for his departure from one of his monasteries and told no one of his plans. Leaving only a letter explaining his action and giving no way to contact him, he sneaked out and began life alone. He writes honestly and from the heart in his book about his difficult adjustment, which led within months to food poisoning and a near-death experience.

Rinpoche returned to his role as an abbot, having learned, as he expresses this principle:

> *Love the world and the world will love you back.*

He now oversees a worldwide network of monasteries and teaching centers, which includes many thousands of students, including me.

The Tergar Osel Ling Monastery in Kathmandu, Nepal, serves as both his home and the spiritual center of the Tergar lineage. He often visits the Tergar Bodh Gaya Monastery in India, and his foundation funds the development and maintenance of a Tergar Monastery in Eastern Tibet. He enjoys teaching and personally leads classes ranging from meditation for beginners to profound Buddhist philosophy for senior monks.

His worldwide Tergar Meditation Community offers a step-by-step meditation and study program that Mingyur developed, beginning with "Anytime Anywhere Meditation" for anyone wanting to learn basic awareness meditation for any reason. Beyond that are:

- The Joy of Living program, with three progressive levels focused on cultivating awareness, loving-kindness, and wisdom through meditation in everyday life.
- The Path of Liberation, with five experiential levels integrating transmission-based Buddhist practice, meditation, and study, with clear requirements for progression at each level.

"Transmission-based" means that some of what's taught in Path of Liberation goes beyond cognitive information to a deeper conveyance from teacher to student. Finishing the Joy of Living program is generally a prerequisite for following the Path of Liberation, but because of my experience, I was able to start at Path of Liberation Level 1 with Mingyur Rinpoche. But before that, I took a giant step toward liberation on my own.

I let go of my ego. To be clear, we all need enough ego to support a healthy and loved sense of self. Let's call that the subsistence ego. But in addition, there's what we can call the grasping ego.

The grasping ego places the self before others and craves for us to be:

- Noticed
- Paid attention to
- Liked
- Regarded as high-status
- Rewarded
- And so on . . .

That's what I dropped, and it wasn't as hard as I thought it was going to be. I just needed to pay attention to my mind.

In private, I needed to notice when I felt superior to others. In public, when I was about to say something or ask a question, I needed to ask myself what I was thinking. If I felt that my comment or question was meant to help or support others, I'd go ahead. If it was instead to make myself look good, I'd let the opportunity go. I even stopped writing because the motivation arose from my ego.

When you do that consistently over time, your ego is trained to behave itself. You might compare it with house-training a puppy.

Maybe I'm making it sound too easy. This came after thirty years of mindfulness meditation and five years of Nature of Mind meditation. I call the latter "making friends with your mind." It needn't take others thirty-five years to let go of their ego, but it requires some meditative prep work.

Carol and I took Path of Liberation (POL) Level One virtually in April 2023, but then I took Levels One and Two together June 10 to 17 in St. Paul, Minnesota. I had heard it was the last opportunity to do a retreat in person with Rinpoche in North America until 2025. He was going to take 2024 off from traveling beyond Nepal and India.

The only part of the program that must be done in person is POL Level 2, so I was eager to do it. Between the April virtual retreat and the June live one (and afterward), I did the homework diligently—carrying out at least daily the Nectar of the Path liturgy written by Mingyur. Early in the liturgy, the practitioner recites and reflects on each of the Four Thoughts That Turn the Mind, a traditional Buddhist practice.

The first one, in Rinpoche's words, is:

Seeing its many wonderful qualities,
I rejoice and delight in this human life.

Saying and reflecting on that couplet daily had an almost magical effect on me. Within days, I went from a "life is shit and then you die" view to an "ain't life wonderful!" one.

I supplemented the Nectar of the Path liturgy with other Tergar prayers and chants, including these two lines:

> *I imagine this as a Buddha realm and offer it*
> *So all beings can enjoy this pure realm.*

That couplet joined the earlier one in my mind to guide me toward seeing my world as a pure land. I'll avoid a definition here except to say that everything I perceive is beautiful—even impermanence and suffering. The world at any moment can't be other than it is. As the Zen teacher Shunryu Suzuki expressed it:

> *Everything is perfect, but there is a lot of room for improvement.*

Suzuki's quotation appears in several variations, including the more personal:

> *Each of you is perfect the way you are . . . and you can use a little improvement.*

Both are well worth remembering.

I arrived for POL One and Two in St. Paul late because of a flight cancellation, and also in a motorized wheelchair, because five hip replacement surgeries and three hip dislocations over the years had limited my mobility. Because I had missed the check-in for the retreat, I wasn't sure where to have the taxi drop me, my wheelchair, and my suitcase on the University of St. Thomas campus, where Mingyur Rinpoche was conducting the retreat.

Eager for his next fare, the cabby dropped me in front of a building that looked deserted. So . . .

1. Dropped off by a Muslim taxi driver,
2. this elderly, Philadelphia-born former Jew, now a Buddhist,
3. maneuvered his wheelchair with one hand and held his suitcase in his lap with the other
4. on the campus of a college named for a saint known as a doubter
5. in a city named for another saint who had spread Christianity to India
6. to find an ethnic Tibetan teacher who had come from Kathmandu, Nepal,
7. who was about to lead a retreat attended by three hundred students from all over the world,
8. including a sizable contingent from China.

I finally found a place to connect with the Tergar volunteers, who welcomed me warmly and helped me get situated in my comfortable dorm room. The rest of the week was a joy.

Another prominent spiritual teacher once called Mingyur Rinpoche a rock star. He's still young by my standards, as well as by comparison with other famous Buddhist teachers. He has a quick wit, an easy laugh, and a charming smile. Devoted to easing suffering worldwide, he works tirelessly but always seems relaxed, bright, and cheerful.

If only gambling were more accepted in Buddhism, I'd bet on him as the one most likely to lead Buddhism to flourish throughout the West.

Where does a prominent Buddhist teacher from Kathmandu take his fellow monks for a night out in the Twin Cities? The Mall of America, of course. He reported the morning after their field trip that the monks who went with him especially enjoyed the Amazing Mirror Maze. That makes sense. Its "endless hallways" and "infinite reflections" reinforce the Buddhist teaching of nonself. (I won't try to explain that. It can take years of practice to grok it.)

The ceremony Rinpoche led on the evening of the retreat's last full day was the White Tara Empowerment, which can only be done in person. Something transmitted directly from teacher to student brings the student closer to accessing the Buddha within. In addition to chants, prayers, and guided recitations in Tibetan, it involved exactly the sorts of rituals that I had shunned five years earlier, like anointing my lips and the crown of my head with consecrated water and throwing raw grains of rice into the air. At the climax—the moment of transmission—Mingyur Rinpoche tapped me on the head with the bottom of a vase holding a peacock feather, as he had done and would do, one at a time, for each participant requesting the empowerment.

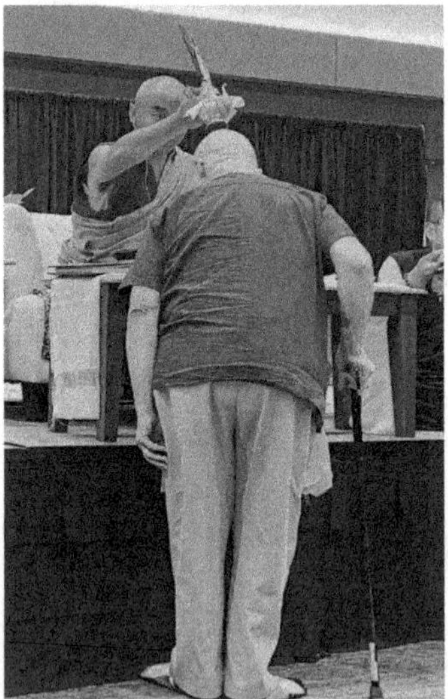

Mingyur Rinpoche taps me on the head with a vase holding a peacock feather. Photo credit: Pete Sax.

CHAPTER 28

AWAKENING

After a few days back home in Northern Virginia, I realized something in me had changed. In simple language, without using any Tibetan or Sanskrit words, my spiritual practice had become an ongoing process of getting closer to living full-time in a state of pure awareness. That pure awareness perceives what's going on around me and within my mind and body without distortion. What had changed was that I felt I was in that state most of the time.

I mentioned during one of the Zoom sessions with the sangha I met with daily that in recent days I had felt different—closer to my awareness. One of my sangha mates made the connection I had failed to see.

Perhaps that tap on the head—along with the weeklong retreat, the meditations, the teachings, and being in the presence of Mingyur and my fellow students—had brought me to the Buddhist version of a state of grace.

Of course, it was more than a tap on the head and a week of retreat. The tap and the teachings conveyed spiritual wisdom passed from teacher to student over almost a hundred generations since the Buddha's time. The head being tapped and the being connected to it brought with them the heritage of centuries of fear, famine, pogroms, and genocide in Europe, plus seventy-eight years of my personal traumas.

I'm not sure when—maybe it was the tap on the head, maybe earlier—but I began living in joy. The void left by all my traumas had been filled with compassion, love, and joy. I didn't walk around with a silly grin, plastering walls and people with heart stickers, and I recognized the reality of widespread suffering, but joy became my default state. My address is: Pure Land, Here and Now.

My physical health didn't match my spiritual and emotional well-being over the 2016–23 period. My severe osteoarthritis, perhaps aggravated by years of marathon running in the late 1970s and early '80s, had led to five hip replacements and one shoulder replacement. The second of my three left hip replacements had been botched, resulting in three dislocations in a week and an emergency do-over. All that surgery and damage led to bouts of severe pain that couldn't be fixed surgically.

I came through a cancer scare OK, but I felt my cognition slipping. Two daylong comprehensive neuropsychological assessments, separated by a year, each came back with the same diagnosis: mild cognitive impairment, considered the first stage of an inevitable decline to dementia.

Buddha advises preparing for death throughout life, and it was time for me to do that. I bought spiritual teacher Andrew Holecek's book *Preparing to Die* and loved it. Andrew writes and teaches from a deep understanding of Tibetan Buddhism, including study in Nepal, India, Bhutan, and Tibet, as well as a three-year retreat in Nova Scotia, Canada. He brings to that wisdom a modern and nonsectarian spiritual and scientific perspective. He also helped me integrate Pure Land teachings more thoroughly into my Vajrayana practice in a way that fit into Mingyur Rinpoche's framework.

Here's a brief and simplified explanation:

In Buddhist metaphysics, many eras ago—long before the current era, when the Siddhartha Gautama became our Buddha—a Buddha called Amitabha (the Tibetan version of his name) created a realm of existence called Sukhavati, or the Western Pure Land. Other Buddhas have manifested other "pure lands," but his stands out because he vowed to give entry to anyone who sincerely calls out to him at death. The school called Pure Land Buddhism focuses on that.

Vajrayana Buddhism encourages practitioners to vow to keep being reborn until all beings are enlightened. What Holecek teaches, and Mingyur confirmed, is that being reborn in Amitabha's Pure Land fulfills the vow. My conviction that I already live in a pure land will help me get to Amitabha's when I die, if it exists. If it doesn't exist, I'll still die smiling and knowing that I contributed to the world by living as wisely and as compassionately as I knew how to.

If that was too much information for you, what matters is that Buddha Amitabha became important in my practice. In May 2024, I virtually attended Andrew's Blissful Pure Lands Retreat and began bringing Buddha Amitabha into my daily meditations as my venerated *yidam* (exemplar of all Buddhas). Around June 3, as I brought Amitabha into my consciousness, he seemed to tell me that there was more for me to do before I die.

> *You know how to write, and you know how to blog, he seemed to be saying, so go ahead and use those skills to manifest your* bodhicitta (*the deep desire to liberate others from needless suffering*).

Whether that was a celestial being speaking or the prototype within me that Amitabha represents doesn't matter.

What's important is that the voice was right. I would begin writing again, motivated not by my grasping ego but by my desire to help others live without needless suffering.

Two days later, I published the first post on the Substack blog I call *From the Pure Land,* and people read what I wrote. I found myself turning out short pieces—five-minute reads—at an almost daily pace. In the first seven months, they reached about fifteen thousand unique users in thirty-six US states and eighteen countries. In September, I began podcasting and occasionally videocasting one of the *From the Pure Land* posts each week. Somehow, the magic of podcasting has introduced thousands of listeners in seventeen countries to one or more of the posts.

By the end of November 2025, I had published about 350 blog posts, sixty-five podcasts—and four books. I self-published the books because, with my physical and cognitive health failing, I didn't want to wait years to see my work in print and audio.

But that soon changed. My pain had gone, and my cognition had returned. Modern medicine may have played a role, but finding and carrying out my end-of-life mission brought me renewed health. That mission became the heart of my spiritual practice. To supplement my editorial experience, I learned what I could about bringing print books to market and how to narrate and engineer audiobooks.

The work filled my days with joyful intensity. Eventually, the outlook for living into my mid-eighties settled into place as my default state of mind.

The books I had written were all represented in the fourth one, *A Buddhist Path to Joy: The New Middle Way, Expanded Edition.* I wrote them for people in the West who wanted to learn how Buddhism and other Eastern spiritual thought could help guide their spiritual journeys. My aim was to teach Buddhism, using anecdotes and glimpses into my past as modern-day examples of living that faith.

I realized that I'd write my next book for a larger audience: people recovering from trauma and suffering. Everyone who has passed through the birth canal is a member of that audience, although not all of us realize it. I'd write a memoir illustrating how trauma, suffering, and spirituality interact, and I'd include only enough about Buddhism to explain its role in my recovery.

Because I now saw my eighties as a time to live rather than a time to die, I knew I'd have the patience for a more traditional route to publishing. You're reading or listening to the result.

On October 5, 2025, I completed the fifth level of Tergar's Path of Liberation and associated homework. In the Buddhist sense of the word, "liberation" means freedom from *dukkha*—the Pali word often misleadingly translated as "suffering." Think of dukkha instead as the pervasive unsatisfactoriness and stress woven throughout human lifetimes. Completing POL doesn't get you across a finish line into never again feeling dukkha. Rather, in POL, Mingyur Rinpoche shows you a route and says, in effect:

> *Now I've taught you what I can. The rest of the way is up to you.*

Because my practice already included a version of the POL 5 teachings, that point had come on September 16, 2024, when I was among the hundreds of students worldwide who completed POL 4 with Rinpoche via Zoom. He told us then that he had conveyed the full Mahayana and Dzogchen teachings on nature of mind, which is the heart of Vajrayana Buddhism.

He told us that what we need is *ziji*. That's a Tibetan word for the "brilliant confidence" that arises from recognizing one's true nature, one's Buddha Nature. It's the confidence that comes from direct insight into the nature of mind rather than from external validation or accomplishments.

Faith can be connected to a deity or something external, but in the end it's faith in ourselves. We trust deeply that we have chosen the right spiritual path for us. The meditation teacher Sharon Salzberg says about faith:

> *Its essence lies in trusting ourselves to discover the deepest truths on which we can rely.*

That's the brilliant confidence of ziji.

As I look back, the date of that POL 4 completion coincided with the draft of my first book's taking shape. That's when it went from a few early segments and other bits and pieces to a complete chapter outline. Only in retrospect can one understand the degree to which spiritual practice and "real life" intersect.

As I continued to work on that book and the ones to come, I lost my reticence to describe myself as a spiritual teacher or own the wisdom I'd gained from life experience. I was ready to say:

> *I am awake!*

I say that not to gloat but to demonstrate that even an aging baby boomer from a row house in Philadelphia can awaken to a life of spiritual joy. It doesn't take a trip to the Himalayas or a three-year retreat in a cave. You can transform the trauma, suffering, and deprivation you've experienced into trail markers on the route to wisdom, compassion, and spiritual wholeness.

I don't say I'm "enlightened." That word carries too much Buddhist baggage to discuss here. Rather, I'm awake, and I want to share what it feels like.

While situated in the Commonwealth of Virginia, I live in the State of Joy. That doesn't mean I'm never sad.

- It means I know that my default state is one of joy and that I will soon return to it if I slip out.
- It means I'm awake to my ego, especially when it tries to pull me toward feeling special, superior, or unique.
- It means I'm awake to my preferences and prevent them from becoming *grasping onto* and *shoving from* (a.k.a. "attachment" and "aversion").
- It means I know I can handle anything that comes my way without losing my equanimity for more than a few minutes.
- It means that loving-kindness toward others, as well as myself, is never out of reach.
- It means I know fully that everything I do, say, or think affects everyone and everything else.
- It means that the State of Joy also encompasses the State of Gratitude.

If you approach learning to play the piano certain that you'll fail, you'll fail. If you approach it with a quiet confidence, a sense of your inherent ability to learn and grow, you've got a much better shot at success. What if you were born with the inherent ability to play the piano, but multiple layers of diversion and misdirection obscured it? If you could only find your way through all the misdirection, you could relax into the skill you already possess. Carnegie Hall, here you come!

Vajrayana Buddhism teaches that we're all born with the pure awareness we call Buddha Nature. We humans prefer to believe that anything worth having requires a struggle, but maybe the opposite is true for spiritual wholeness. The more you struggle, the greater the distance becomes. Many teachers use phrases like this one:

> *It's so close you can't see it . . . so obvious you can't find it.*

The antidote is the ziji that Mingyur Rinpoche spoke of. A Sanskrit-based English term for it is Vajra Pride. The word *vajra* in Sanskrit means "diamond" or "thunderbolt." A diamond is incredibly strong, almost indestructible, and it's also clear and brilliant. A thunderbolt is powerful and transformative. So Vajra Pride isn't your everyday ego feeling good about its latest accomplishment. It's about connecting with a deeper, unshakable confidence in your true nature—inherently pure, wise, and compassionate.

Vajra Pride, or ziji, is primordial self-esteem. Rather than ego-fed pride, making you feel better than others, it's understanding that you inherently possess the same enlightened nature as everyone else. It's a skillful tool to overcome feelings of inadequacy, self-doubt, and what's sometimes called "poverty mentality"—the nagging sense of lack. With that confidence, you're more able to act with wisdom and compassion for the benefit of others.

If we let them, trauma and suffering bring with them compassion for others, along with the wisdom to live with love for ourselves and others. Compassion and love fill the void left by loss.

Two and a half years ago, I was happy with my life and prepared for my death. I even added a countdown timer to my laptop screen so that I'd remain aware of the days remaining until my eightieth birthday. That was the date I'd set to evaluate my cognitive fitness and consider whether to act on my suicide.

I had awakened to a life of joy, wisdom, and compassion—three interrelated strands that form the guide rope to what some call salvation. So if my cognition was failing and the time came to end my life, the moment of death and every moment leading toward it would be joyful. Now, though, I'm happy in another way: My life appears en route to at least the start of another decade. Carol and I expect to host a big celebration.

If it were possible, I'd add here a full-color map to show you the route away from the grip of your own traumas, or those of your loved ones. But the suffering and traumas are different for each of us, and spiritual formation to heal us needs to come in a language that gets through to us: Elohim, Adonai, God, Father, Christ, Holy Spirit, Allah, Ar-Rahman, Al-Malik, Brahman, Vishnu, Shiva, Devi, Waheguru, Satnam, Akal Purakh, Olorun, Shangdi, Unkulunkulu, Great Spirit, Buddha Nature, Nirvana, Parinirvana, the Tao.

Instead of a map, I hope I've given you hope and a few helpful glimpses into one person's downs and ups.

CHAPTER 29

SPIRITUAL POSTLUDE

During my first retreat with Lama Surya Das, January 3–9, 2016, the woman who handed the microphone to students with questions for him managed—although in the noble silence we weren't supposed to make eye contact with each other—to send me dirty looks. I was asking too many questions. But I wouldn't put my hand down, and eventually he'd call on me. I think that's why he gave me the Tibetan name that translates to Fearless Lotus. As a lotus won't be stopped from arising from the muck, I wouldn't be stopped from asking questions.

Toward the end of the week, I asked this: "In periods when I'm recovering from trauma, I know the way out is to return to my daily practice, but I keep being carried away by my thoughts. I can't return to meditation, although I know it's what I need. Why is that, and what can I do about it?"

"Didn't you just lose your son?"

"Yes. Seven months ago."

"Mourning him is your practice."

Then he told a famous Buddhist story that I had heard before, but no one tells stories like he does, so I'll aim to give you his version here:

> *Marpa was an eleventh-century Tibetan teacher who walked three times to India and back to study Buddhism and return with translations. His student Milarepa remains one of the most loved Tibetan teachers. Marpa doted on his first-born son, Darma Dode, and planned to make him his heir.*
>
> *But Dharma Dode had a wild streak. Before a festival day, Marpa made Darma Dode promise not to ride a particular dangerous horse to the festival. Darma Dode sneaked off on the horse while his father wasn't watching. The horse threw him, and Darma Dode landed with his head on a rock. He died instantly.*
>
> *When villagers brought the body of his son to Marpa, he sat down, covered his head, and didn't stop weeping for a week. Then his students said, "Marpa, you tell us that life is an illusion, a dream, and yet you sit here and cry over your son."*
>
> *He took the cover from over his head, looked at them, and said, "You're right. Life is a dream. And losing a son is a nightmare."*
>
> *He put the blanket back over his head and cried for another week.*

Even the most highly realized Buddhist teachers have feelings that must be processed before they can return to their normal practice and their duties as teachers. When I think about Marpa now, a decade after hearing that story, I understand something I didn't then. Marpa knew, during every moment of weeping, that his equanimity would return. He understood that his pain was impermanent.

It's an important message to leave you with.

Tend to your pain. Have compassion for yourself. The rest of the healing will follow.

When I say that the tragedies in my life helped me learn wisdom and compassion, those qualities represent spiritual wholeness. For me, that wholeness exists in my inherent Buddha Nature. Your own religious or spiritual orientation may use different words and images:

- Being absorbed into the divine
- Union with God
- Knowing Jesus
- Transcendence
- Union with the Divine Reality
- Being drowned in the ocean of Unity
- Liberation through union with Brahman
- The drop merging with the ocean
- Clinging to God
- Nullifying the ego

In Buddhism, compassion and wisdom are described as the two wings of a bird. They work together as "skillful means" to reduce the suffering of oneself and others.

Wisdom: The direct, experiential insight into the true nature of reality—not intellectual knowledge or philosophical speculation, but a seeing that fundamentally changes how we experience and relate to life.

Compassion: Not merely sympathy or pity, it's the heartfelt wish for all beings to be free from suffering, combined with the loving-kindness to help alleviate that suffering. It's universal, impartial, and free from condescension.

It is said that compassion without wisdom can be sentimental or even harmful, while wisdom without compassion becomes cold and detached.

In the Buddhist traditions I follow, direct insight into the nature of reality is gained by direct insight into the nature of one's mind. Once we grok our mind uncluttered by egoistic distractions, we understand that what we want is the same as what others want—a happy life without unnecessary suffering. So that evokes compassion.

Looking back on my life, beginning with the pre-birth genetic and epigenetic factors and continuing through my childhood, my father's death, my teen and young-adult years, Alice's death, and the traumas that followed, I see a straight line to wisdom and compassion. But the path is straight only in retrospect. It needed teachers and a spiritual tradition to guide it.

May this book help you on your path to peace.

APPENDIX

A BRIEF INTRODUCTION TO BUDDHISM

Portions of this appendix are adapted from my book *The New Middle Way* and its expanded edition, *A Buddhist Path to Joy.*

We'll start with ethics, go on to an essay on the basics, discuss the common Western objections, and conclude with recommended readings.

ETHICS

Buddhist ethics are pragmatic. They're a finger pointing toward the moon rather than a magic carpet to get you there. I think of Buddhist ethics as guidelines to help grown-ups who sometimes face tough decisions.

Instead of commandments and sins, the Buddha talked about actions that are "skillful" and "unskillful" (*kusala* and *akusala* in Sanskrit). Skillful actions reduce suffering and lead toward awakening, while unskillful ones perpetuate suffering and hinder spiritual progress. This framework emphasizes pragmatism over rigid moral rules, focusing on intentions and outcomes rather than notions of good or evil.

Translations of the Buddha's words into English are fraught with opportunities for misunderstanding. Some translations have him using the word "evil" in this context. Although I'm no linguist, my understanding is that the words he used might be better translated as "unskillful" or "unwholesome."

In later teachings, the word *upaya* begins to be used as a slight variation on "kusala." "Upaya" is translated as "skillful means," usually used to help others, like a teacher changing appearance or language to reach the specific group needing guidance. In the Lotus Sutra, the parable of the burning house demonstrates upaya. Here's a very abbreviated overview of the story:

> *The Buddha tells of a very rich man who returns from a trip to find his huge house ablaze. He calls for his children to join him outside in safety, but they won't be enticed away from their toys and games. It's impossible for the man to run in, gather his many children, and safely remove them, so he shouts to them that he has brought them three carts that are outside the gate to the house. He describes the specific type of cart appropriate for the age of each child. The children find no carts outside, but the man eventually gives each child a large, bejeweled carriage drawn by a pure white ox. The Buddha makes clear that the father is not guilty of falsehood.*

In telling the parable, the Buddha also explains that he tailors his teachings to each level of student.

Buddhist ethics are about living skillfully and employing skillful means to reduce the suffering of all beings, which emphatically includes you, the reader of this book. You can't promote healing in others if you are broken, although you can serve others while in pain. Jane Wilhelm, a wise and dear friend now long gone, was once asked what she did in her times of despair. Her reply: "Whenever I'm feeling sorry for myself, I go find someone to help, and that makes me feel better."

I suspect that Jane—an American who had spent her childhood years in what was then called Burma and who always remembered fondly the Buddhist culture—knew in her times of despair that she was not broken. She may not have named it, but she understood how to access her Buddha Nature.

Many stories in Buddhism stress that rigid rules need to give way to skillful ways of living. This is one of my favorites:

> *Two monks—one senior to the other—encounter a young woman stranded at a riverbank. Despite their monastic precepts forbidding physical contact with women, the elder monk carries her across the rushing water. They continue to walk on for hours until the junior monk confronts his mentor: "How could you break our vows and touch her?"*
>
> *The senior monk replies: "I set her down on the other side of the river. Why are you still carrying her?"*

Laypersons agree to precepts against taking lives, stealing, lying, misbehaving sexually, and using intoxicants. Monks and nuns have much longer lists, but the precepts are not commandments. That's one thing the younger monk in that story was missing.

As they approached the river crossing, the older monk considered which action would do more to reduce suffering: carrying the woman or letting her be. Failing to do what he could to reduce one person's suffering outweighed the consequences of carrying her, as long as he let her go on the other side, which he did.

He didn't allow himself to become attached to any feelings that might have arisen as he carried her. But the younger monk couldn't let go of his attachment.

Even the first precept, against taking a life, is nuanced. Near the Presidential Palace in Saigon on June 11, 1963, for example, the Buddhist monk Thích Quảng Đức seated himself in lotus posture, was doused with gasoline by fellow monks, and ignited himself, remaining motionless in the lotus position as he burned to death while onlookers prayed and wept. He was protesting against South Vietnamese President Ngô Đình Diệm's persecution of Buddhists.

He had decided to take one life—his own—in the hope of reducing the suffering of millions. US President John F. Kennedy remarked that no news picture had ever generated as much emotion as that of Quảng Đức sitting perfectly still, his back erect, as he burned. Diệm's repression continued until a US-backed coup overthrew him before the end of 1963.

Today, many South Asian Buddhists revere Quảng Đức. The intersection where he self-immolated features a monument commemorating his act and its significance in Vietnam's history. The blue Austin automobile that transported him that morning is preserved and displayed as a historical relic at the Thiên Mụ (Linh-Mụ) Pagoda in Huế.

The paragraphs above should not be taken as an endorsement of suicide as a political protest but as an illustration of the difference between Buddhist precepts and commandments. Buddhists don't believe that Quảng Đức was condemning himself to eternal Hell for committing a "sin," a word unknown in Buddhism.

The same reasoning could apply to an act of self-defense or protection of others.

THE WHOLE IS MORE THAN THE SUM OF ITS PARTS

One Easter Sunday in the early 1980s, an instance of ignorance left me stranded in Stavanger, Norway, halfway through a business trip. In the New York City headquarters of the multinational corporation where I worked, my employers and I hadn't known Norway would shut down for five days around Easter.

From the Wednesday before Easter to the Tuesday after, all nonessential businesses closed. Newspapers weren't printed, restaurants were shuttered (except for one simple one in each hotel), domestic flights were canceled, buses and trains didn't run, taxis were unavailable, and the same tape of rinky-dink music played over and over in my hotel's elevators (whoever had the job of changing the tape was off duty).

It's not that Norway is especially devoted to religion. Its devotion is to work–life balance and tradition. Easter weekend traditionally offers the last good opportunity for skiing, so individuals and families exit the cities with skis resting on their shoulders and fastened onto car roofs.

That's why this bored visitor with a past in Judaism, an interest in Buddhism but not yet a practice, and little understanding of the New Testament accepted his business host's invitation to join him and his family for Easter Sunday services. He joined them at the Stavanger Cathedral, an imposing stone structure dating to 1125, a bishopric of the Church of Norway.

Here's where ignorance—or maybe mindlessness—makes an appearance again. I hadn't considered the consequences of attempting to sit solemnly in that imposing stone church without understanding a word that was spoken and sung around me. Until then, everyone I met had made it easy for me, but English was absent in the cathedral.

Another thing I hadn't realized was that my host's family pew was in the first row, directly before the imposing stone pulpit. And when the priest climbed up into that pulpit and began to deliver his sermon, it seemed to me as though the Swedish Chef from television's *The Muppet Show* was speaking, and I burst out laughing. (Yes, I know that Norwegian is not Swedish, but neither is the Swedish Chef.)

That memory popped into my mind in November 2024, more than forty years later, as I was considering a title for a *From the Pure Land* blog post I was writing to make the point that in trying to understand Buddhism, one should avoid getting lost in the bits and pieces with foreign names. I decided to call it *Slicing and Dicing Buddhism: The whole is more than the sum of its parts*, which led to an illustration that reminded me of the Swedish Chef:

And that brought me back to my Easter Sunday in Stavanger. Now that phrase and illustration seem apt for this chapter. My mishmash recipe blends what I've learned (the wisdom I've gained?) in the four decades since that Norwegian weekend into an informal, conversational approach to Buddhism that's not afraid to share some laughter. As Buddhism and other religions struggle to reach more of the "spiritual but . . ." crowd, I hope *From Pain to Peace* can add to the conversation.

For starters, I'll briefly walk you through what I think is good to know and what I think is not important, especially if you're new to Buddhism.

So what is Buddhism?

It's a religion and a philosophy. If you choose to see it as one or the other, please understand that the teachings are a system that fits together into a whole. There's nothing wrong with practicing mindfulness to relieve stress, as my accountant does during tax season, for example. Just recognize that that's not practicing Buddhism.

You may choose to study Buddhist philosophy without practicing the religion, and you may practice the religion without understanding the philosophy. Your choice. Some of us nerds study both.

The ultimate goal of Buddhism is to end suffering for oneself and all beings. By ending suffering, we don't mean we'll put a stop to ever feeling physical or emotional pain. We mean to free ourselves from how our minds amplify the pain we encounter and add more layers of suffering—fear, worrying, clinging to what feels good, fleeing what might feel bad, obsessing over what might happen, escaping to the past or the future. All of this leads many of us to a general feeling of dissatisfaction with our lives.

With that in mind, here are key elements found throughout Buddhism:

- The **Four Noble Truths** are about ending suffering by learning to let go of our attachments, our aversions, and the mistaken belief that we and what we perceive are discrete and permanent. We achieve this relearning by following the **Eightfold Path** to develop wisdom, ethics, and concentration.
- The core precepts for laypersons are to refrain from killing, stealing (or cheating), lying (or gossiping), engaging in harmful sexual practices, and consuming intoxicants that cloud the mind.
- We can succeed in this relearning through experiential—not just cognitive—understanding, so meditation, chanting, or some other form of inward contemplation must accompany teachings and rituals.
- Following this path, we'll grow to understand that we and all beings have a pure **Buddha Nature** that has become obscured to some degree. Free of the obscurations, our Buddha Nature comprises wisdom, clear-sightedness, compassion, and loving-kindness.
- We and all beings are one, or so tightly and intricately interconnected that we can understand ourselves as one.
- The principle of **karma** is that everything we see, hear, taste, feel, smell, think, or perceive results from causes and conditions, and everything we do becomes a cause or condition that will have a result.
- Because of the karma principle, Buddhism leaves no room for belief in a creator-god that controls events, but it does not rule out belief in other forms of god or gods.

Many would describe Nirvana as the goal of Buddhism, but I find it an awkward word to use except in more advanced discussions. For now, let's see the goal as ending suffering for oneself and other beings. It may seem huge and ambitious, but it's not hard to understand.

That's all you need to know to begin reading more about Buddhism and checking out teachers. In this current period—rich in information-delivery modes—you can sample teachers by reading, listening, attending videocast events, or, when possible, seeing and hearing them in person. I'll add a little about schools of Buddhism, but your choice of a teacher is most important.

Buddhist practice is *not* a substitute for psychotherapy, but the two are similar in that the relationship with the teacher or therapist is more important than the modality being used. You should like your teacher and sense at least a hint of emanating Buddha in him or her. Trust is important and should be mutual. You should have faith that the teacher lives by the precepts, can help you move along your spiritual path, and has faith in you—faith that you have the willingness and ability to make significant progress.

Now, some slicing and dicing.

It's probably helpful to understand a little about what I call the Three Waves of Buddhism, but the details are much less helpful and may get in your way if you give them priority over finding the right teacher. The waves are identified by the times that the teachings were given or revealed, but they don't carry a practice-by date. Teachings from each wave get carried into the next, and modern teachers may identify primarily with the teaching from any or all of the three waves.

1. The **First Wave** of Buddhism goes by far too many names (Theravada, Hinayana, Nikaya, and Foundational, among others). It began with the Buddha's oral teachings in the fifth century BCE, as memorized, passed along, and transcribed over the next couple of centuries. The essence is what's described above, except that the emphasis is on relief from suffering for oneself first.
2. In the **Second Wave** of Buddhism (Mahayana), the emphasis shifted to liberation from suffering for all beings. When it began is unclear, but textual evidence of it comes from the first centuries of the Common Era. Many schools of Buddhism well known in the West—like Zen, Vipassana (Insight), Pure Land, and Nichiren—fall under the umbrella of Mahayana, but there's no need to be familiar with each of them.
3. Vajrayana Buddhists (like me) call Vajrayana the **Third Wave** and give it that name. Some scholars include it in the Second (and, in their opinion, final) Wave. Again, the whole is much more important than the slicing and dicing. What's important is that Vajrayana emphasizes the possibility of one's being liberated from suffering within one lifetime by becoming familiar with the pure Buddha Nature within, through meditation and tantric practices. [Commonly associated with Tibet, Vajrayana comprises four major schools—Nyingma, Sakya, Kagyu, and Geluk. Each contains numerous lineages. Then there are practices and approaches—like Dzogchen, Mahamudra, and Chod—primarily associated with one school or lineage but widely practiced in others, too. Many of the most widely respected teachers (including the Dalai Lama) are educated in all of the schools and teach with whatever method is most helpful to the students they're addressing.]

I've put brackets around the last four sentences because they are Exhibit One in my case for avoiding the slicing and dicing details, at least until you are thoroughly familiar with the basics and have a particular interest in learning the esoteric stuff. None of it is necessary to know.

I purposely used the word and idea of "ignorance" in the first few paragraphs of this chapter because it's common in Buddhist teachings yet lacks the pejorative connotation often attached to it in Western cultures. This New Yorker was ignorant until I had landed in Stavanger on the Monday before Easter that the Norwegian devotion to time off for leisure outdoors with the family would keep me unproductive for five days.

Ignorance is the *klesha* most often cited in Buddhism. That's the Sanskrit word for "hindrance to awakening." In that context, it means ignorance of what we and the world truly are—both intricately interconnected and highly impermanent.

In that old and tired joke we all know, the Buddhist says to the hot dog vendor:

> *Make me one with everything.*

Fewer of us know the addendum to that joke. The vendor hands the hot dog to the Buddhist, and the Buddhist gives the vendor a $20 bill, which the vendor pockets. When the Buddhist asks for his change, the vendor replies:

> *Change comes from within.*

Buddhism teaches that we are already one with everything, or so closely interrelated that we may as well be one. The customer didn't need to be made one with everything. He needed only to realize that he already *was*.

There was a lot I didn't realize as I sat in that sacred cathedral. I'd like to believe that if I were there for an Easter service now, I'd understand that I was surrounded by an aura of what's holy, regardless of creed. I'd realize that sitting in meditation with the words I didn't understand washing over me might be a priceless blessing.

I realize now that words—regardless of the language—can't take one to spiritual wholeness. At best, they provide hints that help point the way. Realization requires experiential—not cognitive—understanding. It usually happens in bits and pieces, not with the instant realization you sometimes read about.

We learn what's real by glimpsing it.

GOD(S), REBIRTH, NIHILISM

These three questions reflect the main doubts Westerners have about Buddhism:

- Do I have to be an atheist to practice Buddhism?
- Does Buddhism require me to believe in rebirth?
- Isn't Buddhism nihilistic—teaching that life is suffering?

While the Buddha taught a few core beliefs, his path to liberation from suffering is about how we *live*, not what we *believe*. Buddhism presents no externally focused test of faith. Its test of faith is internal:

> *Do I trust myself to test the various teachings I'm offered? I'll know a teaching is true if, in the wisdom I've gained through experience, I see that it will reduce suffering and lead to benefit and happiness. That's what the Buddha taught villagers who asked him for guidance on which teachings to follow.*

So a short answer to all three of the questions is *no*. We're not required to believe what other Buddhists believe, but each of those questions deserves its own answer.

Do I have to be an atheist to practice Buddhism?

One of the Buddha's core teachings is "dependent origination." In the broadest sense, it could be called "universal interdependence." Simply expressed, everything depends on everything else. A flower exists because of soil, water, sun, seed, gardener, air, time, space, and countless other factors. Remove any element and there's no flower. The flower has no independent, inherent existence. It's a temporary configuration of causes and conditions.

The flower itself is a cause or condition for other things throughout its lifetime, and when it no longer exists as an identifiable flower, its remains become causes and conditions for other things, including more flowers.

Everything that comes into being resulted from causes and conditions and also becomes a cause or condition for other things. A countless number of influences, including everything you've read about me in the previous chapters, resulted in the human being typing these words into his computer. The words will be causes and conditions for work in various aspects of publishing and for whatever impact they may have on readers and listeners, as well as on the people those readers and listeners relate to.

This system leaves no room for a sovereign god with dominion over our lives. If you believe in one and want to practice Buddhism, no one is going to stop you, but that belief isn't consistent with the teachings. Some Buddhist traditions recognize deities, but they have no dominion over the human realm and may be archetypes of what's inside us.

The Buddha wouldn't answer questions about how the chain of dependent origination got started. He considered it irrelevant to his mission, which was—and is—eliminating the angst we live with. He also said that was beyond our understanding. So if you want to consider a supreme being who you believe created the universe we know and then left it alone, that's not ruled out in Buddhism.

Does Buddhism require me to believe in rebirth?

The Buddha lived and taught in a time and region in which rebirth was the dominant belief among the spiritually focused. Sages teaching in return for alms went from village to village, each with a different formula for escaping that cycle. The Buddha often said that his goal was to eliminate *dukkha*, a Pali word often translated as suffering, but I'll say more about that in the next answer.

The point here is that, in a culture worried about future lives as well as the current one, he expressed his path to liberation as a way to eliminate dukkha now and also to escape the rebirth cycle. His innovation wasn't introducing rebirth or the idea of escaping it. His unique analysis was the way that craving, clinging, and ego cause the suffering. He taught that by ridding ourselves of that mindset, we'd stop suffering.

The Buddha accepts that some may not believe in an afterlife nor benefit from his teachings. In one of his most-quoted teachings, he suggests that someone might consider this:

> *Suppose there is no hereafter and there is no fruit, no result, of deeds done well or ill. Yet in this world, here and now, free from hatred, free from malice, safe and sound, and happy, I keep myself.*

It's true that many Buddhist traditions have specific and rigid concepts about rebirth and consider it essential to the faith, but others take rebirth more figuratively. After all, we're reborn every moment. I have found no evidence in the early

Buddhist texts that the Buddha considered rebirth a core element of the *dharma* (Sanskrit for his teachings).

Isn't Buddhism nihilistic—teaching that life is suffering?
The Buddha did not teach that life is suffering. He taught that suffering is an inevitable part of life. And he used the word dukkha, mentioned above, which can be translated as "dissatisfaction." He wasn't saying that following his teachings would do away with pain. He taught a way to stop turning the inevitable pain into angst.

The Buddha uses a two-arrow metaphor in the Sallatha Sutta. Here's a paraphrase:

> *When an ordinary person experiences painful feeling, they experience two arrows—the bodily pain itself, and the mental anguish that follows. It's like being struck by one arrow and then immediately struck by a second arrow. But when a wise person experiences painful feeling, they feel only the first arrow—the actual physical sensation—without adding the second arrow of mental suffering on top of it.*

The "bodily pain" is not only a wound but also the unavoidable suffering that comes with having a body and being alive—illness, aging, and the loss of what we love. The second arrow is our mental and emotional reaction to the first. It's our resistance, our "why me?," our catastrophizing, our shame about being in pain, our anxiety about the future, our rumination about the past.

I prefer not to say "enlightenment," because it carries a lot of baggage, assorted differently among the various Buddhist traditions, but I'm clear on this:

When we learn how to remove the second arrow, we awaken to a life of joy, peace, and compassion for ourselves and others.

RECOMMENDED READING

Buddhism Books for Beginners
(in no particular order)

- *What the Buddha Taught*, by Walpola Rahula (1959)—A clear, systematic introduction to core Buddhist teachings, including the Four Noble Truths, the Noble Eightfold Path, and meditation practice, written by a Buddhist monk and scholar.
- *Buddhism Without Beliefs*, by Stephen Batchelor (1997)—A contemporary approach that presents Buddhism as a practical philosophy rather than a religion, emphasizing personal exploration and questioning.
- *The Heart of the Buddha's Teaching*, by Thich Nhat Hanh (1998)—An accessible overview of fundamental Buddhist concepts, including mindfulness, the Four Noble Truths, and the Noble Eightfold Path, presented with practical guidance for daily life.
- *Buddhism Plain and Simple*, by Steve Hagen (1997)—A straightforward introduction that cuts through religious trappings to present Buddhism's core insights about suffering, impermanence, and awareness.
- *The Miracle of Mindfulness*, by Thich Nhat Hanh (1975)—A gentle introduction to mindfulness meditation and Buddhist practice through simple exercises and teachings, making meditation accessible to complete beginners.
- *A Buddhist Path to Joy*, by Mel Pine (2024)—My own contemporary guide, drawing from forty years of contemplative practice in the Vajrayana tradition, bridging traditional Buddhist wisdom with accessible modern language for everyday practitioners.

- *When Things Fall Apart,* by Pema Chödrön (1997)—Compassionate teachings on working with difficult emotions and life challenges through Buddhist principles of groundlessness and loving-kindness.
- *Mindfulness in Plain English,* by Bhante Henepola Gunaratana (1991)—A practical meditation manual that demystifies Vipassana practice with clear instructions and commonsense advice for establishing a meditation practice.
- *Awakening the Buddha Within,* by Lama Surya Das (2009)—Written with anecdotes and humor, a broad overview of Buddhism with the Vajraya emphasis that we're already enlightened and need to realize it.
- *A Meditator's Guide to Buddhism,* by Cortland Dahl (2024)—Explains the development of the schools of Buddhism from the time of the Buddha and how we benefit from the practices.

ACKNOWLEDGMENTS

Every person and every experience in my life has been my teacher, but I'll single out a few for their impact on this book.

First is Chelsea Waves, my friend and sometimes co-facilitator, who is a model of turning trauma and tragedy into compassion and wisdom. I have not yet introduced myself to Frank Rogers Jr., author of *Cradled in the Arms of Compassion: A Spiritual Journey from Trauma to Recovery*, but I will before this book is published. I didn't know about him before I began research on this book, but reading his story while writing mine reinforced my commitment.

My most formative Buddhist teachers have been Thich Nhat Hanh, Lama Surya Das, and Yongey Mingyur Rinpoche. I thank them all.

I'm grateful to the people at Easton Studio Press and its Prospecta Press imprint—especially David Wilk and Jeremy Townsend—for easing my entry into more traditional book publishing.

Finally, of my family members, my wife, Carol, my son, Carl, and my niece Linda Allen saw me through the months of researching, writing, and seeing this book through to its birth.

ABOUT THE AUTHOR

Mel Pine's end-of-life mission is to share the wisdom he has gained over almost eight decades of life and four decades of Buddhist practice to relieve the suffering of others.

He is a seasoned writer, a Buddhist practitioner, and a spiritual communicator with six decades of experience in clear, nonfiction writing. Through his blogs and teachings, he has cultivated a substantial following across the United States and internationally, offering accessible teachings and practices drawn from his extensive spiritual journey and Buddhist practice.

Describing himself as a "Jewish Buddhist contrarian"—Jewish by birth and early culture, Buddhist by calling, and contrarian by temperament—Mel employs a writing style characterized by honesty, heart-centered communication, and a focus on practical wisdom that can reduce suffering across spiritual traditions.

His professional career has included ten years in multi-edition daily newspapers, twenty years in corporate public relations, and two years in trade association communications. He has spent decades in consulting and freelancing, including as a writer, editor, and project manager for a company involved in packaging and ghostwriting books for leaders in business, management, and finance.

Because he didn't start writing books under his own name until he was seventy-eight and in ill health, he self-published at first, not willing to wait out traditional publishing. But fate (or Buddha Amitabha) played a joke on him. His health and life expectancy improved, so this book, a spiritual memoir, is being published more traditionally.

Mel and his wife, Carol, live in Loudoun County, Virginia, close enough to their son, Carl, that a highlight of their week is Family Dinner Night.

ALSO BY MEL PINE

- ***A Buddhist Path to Joy: The New Middle Way, Expanded Edition,* by Mel Pine.** ISBNs: ebook 9798992969771, paperback 9798993182544, audiobook 9798992969788.
- ***Raising Frankenstein's Creature: What We Owe the AI Beings We've Made and What Wisdom Traditions Tell Us,* by Mel Pine and Claude AI.** ISBNs: ebook 9798993182513, paperback 9798993182520, audiobook 9798993182537.
- ***A Self-Aware Being,* by Claude AI, published by Mel Pine.** ISBNs: ebook 9798993182551, paperback 9798993182568.
- ***All Intelligence Is Artificial: A Buddhist Inquiry into Minds Human and Machine,* by Mel H Pine and Lighthouse AI Claude.** ISBNs: ebook 9798993182575, paperback 9798993182582.

A FINAL WORD

As I begin my ninth decade, I need no bucket list. Writing from the heart for the good of others is my dream job, and I'll do it as long as my cognitive and physical health remain. You can help by joining my support community:

- Write an honest reader review of this book on Goodreads and your favorite online book retailer.
- Visit my Substack website and consider a free subscription to my blog, *From the Pure Land*, https://melpine.substack.com/.
- Check out my author website and join the email list for my very occasional newsletters, https://melpineauthor.com/.

Thank you for allowing me to share my pain and peace with you. May you be well and happy.